Dupe of Being

EDITION
LAFAYETTE

1952

Dupe of Being

Edited by
Roland Hagenberg

PHOTOCREDITS

Cover: Appel painting from helicopter, 1958, Zestienhoven.

Karel Appel. Dupe of Being
Edited by Roland Hagenberg
© 1989 Edition Lafayette
© text by the authors
© photographs by the photographers

Text Vivien Raynor © 1986 NY Times

Concept and design: Roland Hagenberg
Translations from the French: Richard Miller, John Shapley and
Eleonore Speckens
Copy editors: Abigail Esman, Margot Mifflin and Mark Deary
Type: ANY Phototype, New York
Printed by Becker Graphics, New York
In addition a limited edition of 100 books with a signed and numbered
color lithograph by Karel Appel has been published.

Side by side with the human race there runs another race of beings, the inhuman ones, the race of artists who, goaded by unknown impulses, take the lifeless mass of humanity and by the fever and ferment with which they imbue it turn this soggy dough into bread and the bread into wine and the wine into song. Out of the dead compost and the inert slag they breed a song that contaminates. I see this other race of individuals ransacking the universe, turning everything upside down, their feet always moving in blood and tears, their hands always empty, always clutching and grasping for the beyond, for the god out of reach: slaying everything within reach in order to quiet the monster that gnaws at their vitals. I see that when they tear their hair with the effort to comprehend, to seize this forever unattainable, I see that when they bellow like crazed beasts and rip and gore, I see that this is right, that there is no other path to pursue. A man who belongs to this race must stand up on the high place with gibberish in his mouth and rip out his entrails. It is right and just, because he must! And anything that falls short of this frightening spectacle, anything less shuddering, less terrifying, less mad, less intoxicated, less contaminating, is not art. The rest is counterfeit. The rest is human. The rest belongs to life and lifelessness.

—Henry Miller, *Tropic of Cancer*

Contributing writers:

ALAN BOWNESS
CHRISTIAN DOTREMONT
ELEANOR FLOMENHAFT
RUDI FUCHS
ALLEN GINSBERG
SAM HUNTER
RASAAD JAMIE
MARIETTE JOSEPHUS-JITTA
DONALD KUSPIT
LUCEBERT
STEPHANE LUPASCO
RUPERT MARTIN
MARSHALL McLUHAN
VIVIEN RAYNOR
HERBERT READ
PIERRE RESTANY
WILLEM SANDBERG
BERT SCHIERBEEK
MICHEL TAPIÉ
JAN VRIJMAN

Appel exhibition opening speech by Lucebert, 1951.

APPEL'S TOTAL ADVENTURE
by Michel Tapié

1950

Michel Tapié with his portrait, Paris, 1963.

Karel Appel, 1953

The great epic of modern painting, from Impressionism to Dada, touched upon all the various sectors of classical aesthetics, subjecting each to rigorous examination, exhausting each, and producing as its end result a continuous series of unique and unrepeatable masterpieces that lay the question to rest for all time. Dada was both the culmination and the implacable and fecund *tabula rasa* for those who, since then and now, possessed sufficient strength to grasp the whole of its content and to strive towards a new climate for the new era it ushered in.

And although it was normal in the course of all those upheavals to remain on guard against such classical notions, which had to be transcended eventually, the same old clichés have actually been with us for far too long already, attempting to convince us of the virtue of beating down already open doors and confronting the figments of overheated minds or, all too often, trying to make us believe that defiance is only an alibi for total impotence. It is equally normal to maintain that the climate of our present is particularly favorable to the eclosion — rather than the explosion — of real Individuals bearing new and lucid messages about the pressing need of problems other than the current one that is and will be theirs. Appel is one of these, to the highest power. But let no one be misled; such individuals are always very few and far between, and aping them or using them to construct new "isms" are pursuits that are doomed to failure.

If we want a current general term to classify Appel, the one that first springs to mind is the very one that has remained the least defined, the most open-ended and certainly the most anarchically a classical, namely, Expressionism. After Van Gogh, Rouault (I'm thinking in particular of his reincarnations of Père Ubu), Kirchner and the very-much-present Dubuffet, we see in Appel the work produced by a temperament capable of forcefully translating the whole interior cosmography of the human tragedy, directly and deeply, using the entire gamut, devoid of any purism, of any restrictive system, giving rein to every opportunity for the subtlest violence, the most complex evidence.

Such artists forge ahead with a kind of calm that is the result of the total juncture of the force of inertia and expression, silent because all is in their work. Thus it is hard to speak of Appel's work, which I see as the moving and radiant dawning of a new star of the first magnitude, so close to us that it surrounds us with the richness of its dizzyingly euphoric and fruitful rays, creating a plenitude made up of Dionysiac intoxication and the mysterious depths of the human tragedy.

Let us try to sort out the complex reality of Appel's expressed world. His pure colors? From red to black, taking in Veronese green, but so subtly employed, for his world evokes a long, knowledgeable development, not harsh rawness; and we also have that touch of the indefinable that draws us away from the tired old smudges of the virtuoso palette. Appel's pan-wisdom adapts to mystery as if it were something familiar. His subjects? People, animals, birds, flowers. But a human figure may be a mythical hound, a flower a sun (and here I cannot help but think of Van Gogh, with whom — in a self-portrait as well as in a sunflower — we feel that we are at the core of the essential workings of some living star. The subject cedes place to meaning and, sacrificing nothing of his coloral message, Appel reduces his world to freely revealed signs, signs invented in the heat of the adventurous execution of his work. Dada is now more than thirty years old; that's a lot on the scale of the present. Many things have happened in the interim, things that were probably ineluctably necessary, but so unessential that I do not believe any history worthy of the name will retain many of them: various spectacularly neo-Romantic attitudes of which far too much has been said, and all the other neos: neo-classicism, neo-plasticism, neo-realism; so much energy and time wasted over all those fake movements, the refuge of mediocrities aspiring only to become members of flocks as little apt for artistic adventure as possible since Dada brought to a close the revolutionary period of "isms," which in their day engendered works that were epic but that are now firmly relegated to the museums.

The time for experimental works is over, our era can be truly interested only in the few outstanding figures able to create complete bodies of work whose message is total, in which the scale of methods and inventions is indefinitely vast and complex, forcing us to face up to a plenitude as new as it is necessary. Taking the work of Appel and a few other persons as rare but as individual as he (he likes Dubuffet, Mathieu and Etienne-Martin), it is now possible to elaborate an aesthetics worthy of our present—that is, of works that are essentially contemporary and also of ideas that are totally separate from present-day sciences and philosophies. And it is only here that we can say that the adventure is still going on, i.e., that if any authentic pioneers of Karel Appel's calibre exist, they will also manage to find a postulate for Becoming that suits them.

Drawing, 1948, ink on paper

Gouache, 1961, oilstick on paper

THE APPEL AFFAIR
by Christian Dotremont

1950

Drawing, 1949

Hardly has the "Stedelijk Museum Affair" ended than the "Appel Affair" has aroused considerable feeling in Amsterdam. Our friend Karel Appel, a member of the Dutch experimental group, had decorated, not without the consent of the competent committee, one of the walls of the dining hall in the Amsterdam Community Center. Needless to say, his "decoration" was in no way "decorative." As I said, he is a member of the Dutch experimental group. As the competent committee should have expected, Appel created something of violence, but a just, popular violence: Appel comes from the people, and he's not trying to create some old-fashioned Surrealist-type scandal.

However, the officials who met for lunch in the Center's restaurant lost their appetites at the sight of Appel's "beseeching children," and requested the Amsterdam City Council, to which some of them belonged, to take a hand.

The City Council didn't dare have the fresco taken off the wall but instead had it covered with wood. It gagged the "beseeching children."

The architect Van Eyck, who is both a member of the competent committee and of the experimental group, was of a different opinion: standing guard before the revolutionary fresco, he, like the Dutch issue of *Cobra*, said things that shocked the highly placed diners, one of the aldermen turning quite red with rage as a result. He then put out a long and unusually precise pamphlet, *Een Appel aan de verbeelding*, in which he wrote, *inter alia*: "Appel, this type of person doesn't want anything to do with your 'beseeching children.' "

As for us, we make so bold as to advise the Amsterdam City Council to address itself (with Benelux assistance) to the group of "realist-socialist" fresco painters in Brussels who go around saying that experimental art is nothing but an ideological ploy of the reactionary bourgeoisie. The "realist-socialist" fresco painters won't cause them any problems. Ah, councillors, the "beseeching children" may possibly have a book by Laurent Casanova concealed beneath their tattered cloths, but they won't spoil your appetites with the awful stare of poverty, with their terrible despairing hope. With the "realist-socialist" muralists, the "beseeching children" won't be asking for something to eat, they'll be too busy wondering about the role of the subject in painting.

With Aldo van Eyck

Walking Through the Falling City, 1982, 76 × 88″, oil on canvas

APPEL
by Christian Dotremont

1950

Appel has no inferiority complex, nor do his pictures. I don't mean that either he or his pictures are conceited. No, far from it; but they do make their presence known with a certain brutality that leaves small room for doubt. At the very least, we know that Appel exists, that Appel's pictures exist, and that Appel is alive, and that Appel's pictures are made out of real paint, real color. That is undeniable. Everyone agrees on that point.

Appel's painting is obvious painting, but I don't go along with him when, in an attempt to prove that his paintings are materialistic, he invites you to touch their irregular surfaces, to feel their capricious roughness. Those are only apparent evidences of the materiality of Appel and his painting. There are painters who attach the same appearance to their pictures, but they aren't materialists.

Appel's painting is totally materialist, through and through, in what it offers us ostentatiously and in what it offers us with finesse. So that, in it, surface and depth are the same thing. But never say that Appel is brutal and only brutal. Do you say that a man who happens to have a paunch is only a paunch? Only in jest. Appel is a poet whose spontaneity allows none of its aggressive force, its power to shock, to dissipate between hand and canvas.

We are a long way from confectioned art, from artistic candy-making. Appel creates in bulk, and it's not candy.

Appel's rich, after all. Not richer than anyone else...Indeed, what difference does it make, except that he keeps all his wealth at hand, he doesn't use safe-deposit boxes or acetylene torches, and he's generous to boot. We're a long way from the miserly art of so many painters, who give us only one picture per picture, like putting one candle in a candlestick.

He came from the working class and he's remained working class. He hasn't felt impelled to depict poverty, but has preferred to show the pleasures of the world and the joys of feeling (which are indissolubly bound up together) because the working classes have a right to them just as much as anyone else.

(Copenhagen)

Drawing, 1952, ink on paper

Bowling in Amsterdam, 1963.
With R. Campert, Ilse Vinkenoog, Hugo Claus.

APPEL, PAINTER OF LIFE
by Stéphane Lupasco

1961

With Liselotte Höhs, Venice, 1964.

Nothing is more solitary, more obscure than life, and yet nothing is more complicated and more dazzling.

Appel is a painter of life. His wide torrents of vivid colors bend every straight line, bog down geometry in their oily intensity, in the multiformed proliferation of attempts, whirling and smashed.

Whirling, broken... "I smash happenstance," Appel told me, probably unaware of the full import of his intuitive procedure. "I throw on some red, I cut it with black, I smash the happenstance of blue with blue, white with white... Everything's here, you can see it, antagonism and antagonisms of antagonisms and, oddly enough, it all comes together." By which he means an overall dynamic system, a unique individuality.

Whirling, broken, indeed, for what is being propelled from within, what energy brings about, are exclusions turned in upon themselves, one on top of the other, as if to drag each other down, destroy each other, and yet falling into place not only because of this warfare but also because of the deadly aggression, the polychromatic radiance, the light, all around and among themselves.

What we see and what Appel squeezes with thick tubes onto the white canvas is what is brought up from the depths and forced to the surface, this invisible and powerful insurrection determined to triumph over death's spell. Against the attack of the photons, brought on by the forces of annihilation and progressive entropy, Appel's painting draws up a battle plan, opposes the strategy of the dark cybernetic forces unleashing heterogeneous violence and the inseparable enmities of unpredictable creation.

Such a beautiful flow of colors is threatened, crushed. And who would have thought that so many fusings, streams and rivers, with their sparkling masses, who would ever have thought there were such solitudes upon solitudes volcanically built up, and even more solitary, as these morphogeneses, of whose meaning — unless we invent one in the metaphysical delirium of some rapt schizophrenic — we can glimpse only this strange enchantment created by the dynamics of tumult and the arborescences of carnage.

We understand it better when Appel turns to portraiture, when he creates, in his words, "heads in storms that are more like brainstorms in one's head", creating what we call monsters. He plunges behind the symmetrical and harmonious façade of perceptive logic and comes up with the lines of force of macromolecular aggregates whose ineluctable and fatal law is constant dissymetry and disequilibrium.

Appel is the painter of the infra-vital, the infra-carnal, whose intensely vivid colors are like the enemy, the principle of its very being, demanded by life's shadowy parturition.

If I had to come up with a universe inverse to our own, one derived from my own logical deductions gathered, for years now, from energy itself, one that is already being created in laboratories, that anti-universe (which, for certain so far unpublished reasons that I find plausible, is biological) would find in Appel's canvases — and in Michaux's poems and drawings — the illustration of its stars and planets, its galaxies upon galaxies of *living* galaxies.

In Appel's portraits and heads, however, other configurations, another energy-matter

Drawing, 1980, ink on paper

universe, seem to spring into painful life, through those eyes that pierce through the boiling surface of the paint, through the twisted mouths, the misshapen ears and noses, all of them no more than guessed at beneath the colloidal metabolic upheaval.

This, then, is where the artist finds his support, where he takes in his blood, in this primal mind, this whirlwind of heads. Of all men, whatever their field may be, only one can reverse the ineluctable current that tends towards the resolution of conflicts: the artist. The work of art must receive its breathless or throbbing impetus, subtle and unconscious as it may be, from that unthinkable contradiction. It has been said time and again that the real criteria for talent resides in authenticity, but in the authenticity of this contradiction that truly devastates the artist. The artist in words, the musician, the painter . . . And perhaps even more clearly in music, as in so-called abstract plastic creations. The great masters of the past had the theme of religion,* either for struggling against or as inspiration, to provide them with this determining functional substructure of contradictory, antagonistic, dynamism. For figurative art, however, there was and still is the temptation — yielded to by sensual realism and Impressionism — to abandon oneself to the downhill slope of contradiction to the very depths of some ultimate, blessed dissolution.

Such is the dramatic process that is the primary distinctive mark of decorative and abstract art.

And yet, after all, why is this logic — for it is one, despite what professors of the subject may say — of the contradictory a motive force in all works of art? Precisely because it is unthinkable — or at least it always has been, and it will remain so until there is some revolutionary change in our understanding.

Among all the goals the human mind sets for itself, because of some despotic ideal and without going into non-contradiction, this is one of the most insidious and bizarre: to eradicate this affectivity that is so much a part of our very being, this whole range of pleasures and sufferings, emotions and feelings, radically ineffable, which culminate in the tortured pleasure and corrosive happiness we call love. Of all our feelings, without exception, it is the only one that is unlike all the others, the only one that is nothing but itself, the only one that, in order to come into being, need be nothing other than what it is.

And, through a kind of unimaginable grace,

it springs from contradiction. In the last analysis, everything Appel splashes onto his biotic canvases, as if in the throes of a mental orgasm, is chosen to represent the ontological mystery of affectivity, before which we can only utter these almost tautological words: "I love it" — a love that brooks no discussion.

And, once again, why? Nobody knows. Because at that point — and we must reach it, Appel already has — there is no why.

Drawing, 1949

---

* In the end, every religion, if one thinks about it, is a supreme tragedy.

Bert Schierbeek, 1967

THE ANIMAL DRAWN MAN
by Bert Schierbeek

so sometimes we used to come home late at
    night
after having spent the whole day at the foot of
    the rock face
drawing in the animal that has regularly ap-
    peared
to us in dreams throughout our life and that we
    believed
had engraved its shape and motion in our
    minds along with
the need
to trace materially an echo of its appearance so
    that
forever we would know. . .
but what happened?
under our groping fingers, seeking the shape of
    the animal as

he lived in our eyes and our desire to reproduce
    him just
as we saw him, his size and shape seemed to
    increase
to such proportions that the rock face we had
chosen
to contain his apparition seemed to shrivel
    beneath our drawing hands
faster than we could work and the beast could
    be completed
so what were we doing?
were we representing an animal larger than we
    had
ever seen
or was the beast in your eyes larger than the
    rock wall
that we knew to be the largest one in our part of
    the country?
for all our efforts to limit the animal to a
    reasonable
size
so that we could sculpt it into rock were in
vain
so for days on end sitting in a circle we sang
for days and nights
a pre-dawn song
because morning was beginning but not man
one before the end of the afternoon

because the afternoon passes but not man
one before deepest night
when the animal comes alive and takes shape
and after seven days and seven nights what did
  we find?
something we'd never seen before, something
  we'd never known
we couldn't recognize the animal we thought
  we had
known
on the cliff's surface — during the final night
  of our singing
and as if the clear, luminous intoxication of
  fatigue
had opened and sharpened our eyes into tiny
  cold sickles
we saw it move on the surface of the rock in
  clear lines
and it had shrunk and its outline was bright as
  if it
were on fire but with a blue light its enormous
  tail
was like the tongue of a venomous snake and
  through its muzzle it inhaled
white lines that remained stuck to the wall
our song broke off in a stifled cry
the animal was drawing itself
many ran away

and we never saw them again
but those of us who remained silent and
   watched until the night was over
saw the animal's jaws moving
until dawn and as the light grew
its movements slowed and its eyes grew pale
its powerful paws flexed as though it felt itself
   being
drawn towards a place where it knew it would
die for it was nothing more than a dreadful
   spectre
as long as we could perceive it as a dying
   animal
seemingly being absorbed into the rock face
   without leaving the slightest
trace of its terrifying life. . .
until the moment when some of us got up the
   courage to go near
the wall and there we saw, standing against the
   rock as
we had stood for days on end with our chisels
   and our picks and
our scrapers:
the animal drawn man

Drawing, 1980, ink on paper

With Willem Sandberg, 1961.

APPEL AND THE AVANT-GARDE
by Willem Sandberg

1969

The COBRA group enters the Stedelijk Museum, Amsterdam, 1949

66 **A** ppel's work is the premonition and the precursor of that revolt and will to live typical of youth; the cultural experiment prevails over the social experiment, freeing and giving form to a new way of thinking. And that is what avant-garde means."

ART'S REPLY

After the war
I wondered
what art's reply
to all the violence would be
to all these radical changes
in human relations
famous artists barely responded
I was on the point of giving up
when I spied a group of youngsters
who had something to say
and who were saying it in a new voice
violently
maybe even primitively
they were seeking a new language
heatedly
resolutely
Appel was one of their leaders

a world of monsters
churning convulsively
shouting beating rending and rent
strong and benevolent
sprang up under his hands
no going back
paintings sculptures relief object
red black blue and white
canvas ceramic and wood
bearing the hot imprint
and gesture
of a man on the move
Appel found his world
in the convulsive twist of olive trees
their strength attracted him
his axe transformed them
his colors revived them
to give this reply

THE BODY OF APPEL'S WORK IS ALIVE
by Lucebert

1950

With Lucebert, Amsterdam, 1948.

Drawing, 1952, ink on paper

C anvases like clenched fists, masses of pictorial matter like rivers of lava, colors that conquer and rape the eye, sexuality, vitality, a "painting cat running wild": is that Karel Appel?

The Orlando Furioso of painting, a slapdash dervish, the leader of a color mafia, the "brutal blond" of ultra-macho Expressionism?

A tyrant angrily mixing and subduing paint, subjecting pigments to a violence hitherto unheard of in art's long history, a despot who "triumphs," as the phrase goes, over his material?

A color Titan?

There are those who do not even look at Appel, who do not appreciate him or reject him because of the way he unleashes his *furia picturale*, but doesn't that simplistic view reflect a prejudice, a tiny error, even a certain ignorance?

Isn't it true that the man who, outwardly, seems able to move mountains often turns out to be someone whose life is spent in persistently and tirelessly climbing them? Isn't Appel, like so many other modern artists, really just content to be a laborer, devoted and patient, even to the point of passivity, delighted to trade his personal freedom of action against the wisdom of his material? Obviously, Appel is not trying to dematerialize the substance of which his pictures are made, nor to reveal a deep meaning in the perception of physical objects in order to use that meaning to state certain immaterial values of matter and motif. No, he isn't looking for an extra-phenomenal world, for the idea hidden behind natural umber or iron oxide or some "still life with skull." No, his only reference point is the pictorial substance itself. A principle based on realism, on modesty, on modesty and realism, to such a degree that the artist no longer makes the slightest effort to turn the pictorial material into something other than what it is. Appel does not try to impose anything on matter, he does not want to enslave painting; on the contrary he only wants to submit to it himself, obedient to a logic he himself does not possess. And to do that one must have eyes that are open, wide open, unprejudiced, perceptive.

When our minds accept a fact, a truth, we

say that our eyes have been opened. Indeed, how rarely it happens in reality. We are all more or less blind men who can see. And just as our intellectual and sensual universe consists to a large degree of a ceaseless succession of associations that constantly and confusedly blend together, so our visual universe too is a blurred world that is continually fading. We nearly always see a color — a red, for example — as if seeing a better or worse red at the same time or, what is more surprising, we have a tendency to perceive the given red as if there were a blue more yellow than the white of this red, and so on. For most of us, the pure, frank sight of that red red would be torture. We turn away from red and from all colors like we turn away from our dreams.

With an eye that is as impartial as it is attentive, a painter of Appel's quality accepts everything colors have to say to him, he accepts it without unrequited desires or qualifications, he allows the red, the blue, the black to speak as only they know how. Yes, even red has a right to say what it wants, red should not be silenced, even if it shocks us. Let it shout, it may have grounds for doing so, for isn't it often in conflict with its neighbor, green?

Thus, Appel's canvases do not "transcend

Gouache, 1952, on paper

their material," but are replete with it. Indeed, we may wonder how we would classify a canvas that wasn't "full of paint." As soap, toothpaste, frog's eggs or some miracle cream? No, such a canvas is imbued with the spirituality of a refined and purified artistic pleasure. It is, to put it another way, a picture taken by a blind photographer, a slide projected onto the screen of a cloudless sky.

In Appel there is no vagueness, no wispy metaphysics. With each picture Appel actually engages in a reexamination of its particular circulatory system, and such an operation prohibits any vagueness, any wavering, any pretention — and to Appel less than anyone else, given his fondness for painting with a palette knife. Careful with that knife — careful! If it were used haphazardly it could slice an artery, the picture would bleed to death and become a living corpse. And that must never happen! Let it breathe, let its pulse race, allow it to reveal its vulnerability and show itself in all its nakedness, its body firm and moist with shadows, let it have its own will, its own opinions, its own desire. Let it become what it is attempting to be; one day the picture will paint a picture too, by itself if it must, but preferably in the eyes of others. The pictorial body is alive.

Gouache, 1952, ink on paper

Drawing, 1950, ink on paper

ANGER IN THE ATTIC AND BESEECHING CHILDREN

The golden tee-shirt cost millions
And the bronze despot's head has taken even
    God's tinkling mass bell
But that's all behind us now
Today a wig costs as much as real hair

And evening falls. You close ship, pull down
The iron shutters and for a second stare down
    at a puddle
On the sidewalk: "What a wonderful white
    animal"
And then you turn out the lights, except for the
    one over the mirror
And the basket of fruit, fruits that have been
    there for ages
Paris' apple, Bacchus' grapes, Loki's hard
Walnuts, and suddenly you speak clearly,

Think about tomorrow, touch bare wood
And finally remove the iron heating up in your
    head from the fire

The pendulum swings
The centuries roll by, one after the other, the
    dogs dirty the booted foot of the cross
The mouse labors and brings forth the moun-
    tain's rocky tail
Everybody has crept under his tea cosy be-
    tween the two lukewarm radio tubes

But you've moved into the attic, close to the sun
And to the light that has just put a limit on
our thousand and one painters of national still-
    lifes
And there you've made a tree out of washer
    paddles

To set up a friendly racket, one earlier
Made only by those visionary sea birds
The Irish are so fond of
And you've created a path out of scrap
A way for the children to follow
Holding hands with the rag fairies

So:
Among boxes of enough paper clips
To hold together every Montgomery Ward
And Bethlehem Steel stock

Among bags stuffed full of enough harmonicas
To play everything from dawn to dusk, soup to
    nuts,
Among shipments of pocket mirrors, bars of
    soap, yeast

Corks skimmers umbrellas chalk knives
Toy cars revolving lawn-sprinklers pipe-
    cleaners
Newton's rings
Academic busts taxidermized intestines soda
    straws
You extract from life all the intertwined colors
All the colors that break apart

Now you know what red does
Red likes to run through green grass
Now you know what yellow knows
The sun shines because no one wants to die
And as for blue: sky-blue seems black
to the child who is given nothing

Sam Hunter

KAREL APPEL IN THE SPIRIT
OF OUR TIME
by Sam Hunter

1986

The gripping and fantastic imagery of Karel Appel apposite to the 1940s is sustained in recent painting and sculpture, affirmative but rooted in the expressionist conviction of the intense struggle of contemporary life.

Drawing, 1948, ink on paper

In one of his many pointed and laconic statements made during this interesting postwar period, Karel Appel gave us his personal version of "the tradition of the new," with its special European resonance and unique cultural configuration: "To paint is to destroy what preceded it."[2] This important artistic Dutch pioneer was, of course, a founding member, with the Danish painter Asger Jorn and the Belgian poet Christian Dotremont, of Cobra. He was also mainly responsible for bringing the emerging expressionist avant-garde in Holland into contact with their Danish and Belgian counterparts. At the time he made his statement in 1948, Appel had not yet arrived at his familiar and lavish painterly style, but was experimenting with rather stiff, painted constructions reminiscent of the style of Schwitters whose postwar exhibitions in Amsterdam deeply interested him. Appel was instead creating *objets poubelles* (rubbish objects), physically related to, but spiritually quite at cross purposes with, the junk culture of the sixties and the encased, plasticized trash yet to be invented by Arman and the New Realists. Appel's depicted junk and found objects usually centered around a far more poignant and characteristically expressionist theme. In the construction *The Questioning Children* (1949), effigies of children of a Klee-like naivete, and also reminiscent of the American Indian kachina dolls Max Ernst came to admire and collect during the war, were stacked up on brightly painted wood blocks nailed to a board; they seemed to confront a brutilized and hypocritical adult audience with the tragic waste of innocent lives, whether by force of arms or other means of oppression devised by a cruel and unrelenting society bent on self-destruction. Only one year later, in his *Child with Birds* (1950)—the first of a number of Appel paintings to enter the collection of the Museum of Modern Art—the artist had broken away from the perhaps strained social critique and poignancy of his construction phase to achieve a more individualized and complex scenario depicting an equally affecting creational world of predatory aggressors and their prey. Somewhat reminiscent of Picasso, these first mature Cobra works achieved an entirely individual vision in their strangely exhilarating combination of vivid primary color, thick impasto, and virulent subject matter bordering on the grotesque. At the same time, primitivist expression was fused significantly with a loaded brushstroke and gestural abstraction.

Formed on July 16, 1948, the Cobra group echoed Dubuffet's methods for he, too, turned to the art of children, and also the work of the mentally disturbed and the artistically untutored not only for subject matter but as plastic models. Duffet collected the primitivist art of the artistically naive under the rubric *Art Brut*, making their eccentric expressions the basis for his own sometimes hilarious and more often terrifying, caricaturing, paint-laden style of the mid- and late forties Appel may have been directly influenced by Dubuffet when he visited Paris in 1947, where he saw his work exhibited. Like Dubuffet, Appel and the Cobra artist rejected the enlightened and rationalist Western past, momentarily shelving their faith in reason, following the destruction of civilized values in World War II (and thus echoing the Dadaist response after World War I). Also, like Dubuffet and Giacometti and Bacon as well, the Cobra pursued astonishingly diverse formal explorations to comment eloquently and pointedly upon the human situation rather than upon abstract pictorial values, which had so oppressively dominated the post-Mondrian, Constructivist era in Europe in the late thirties. Another Cobra pioneer, the Dutch painter Constant, wrote: "We were aware that we had cut ourselves off from the past and enjoyed unfettered freedom. Only primitive people, children, and psychopaths could reckon on our sympathy."[3]

When the Cobra artists held their first significant, large-scale exhibition in Amsterdam the following year at the Stedelijk Museum, a show organized by Willem Sandberg, the museum's spirited and fearless director, it was treated by both sponsor and participants as a confrontation with an apathetic public. Fiery, defiant assertions were hung on the wall next to the array of crude effigy figures painted in brilliant color and applied in a deliberately childlike manner, daubed in thick, sand-choked pigment. In an introduction some years later to a retrospection exhibition catalogue, *Cobra and Contrasts, The Lydia and Henry Lewis Winston Collection* (Dr. and Mrs. Barnett Malbin), held at the Detroit Institute of Arts in 1974, Sandberg characteristically used free verse and lower case lettering to extol his

discovery during the heady postwar years of
the ebullient new European avant-garde:
I stayed on the lookout
eagerly followed the experiments of youngsters
in search for the reflex of the war. . .
corneille and appel came to see me
told about the new group
founded in paris
check terrace near notre dame
Artists from occupied capitals
COpenhagen BRussels Amsterdam (COB-
RA)
wanted to demonstrate together
their spontaneous vitality
next fall in the stedelijk:
the first COBRA show!
when the exhibition was mounted
I felt enchanted:
red roaring beasts black monsters
shouting from museum walls
lightening visitors
who had come to enjoy "fine arts"
a black cage at the entrance
hung with manifestoes by writers
outcries of poets against the establishment
infuriated the critics
newspaper headlines

strongly decried the scandal:

"insanity extolled as art!"

"tumult in a museum   "[4]

·Among the artists' statements boldly inscribed on the museum walls off found predictable expressions of a utopian vision, and the messianic confidence in a better day soon to appear: "Our art is the art of a revolutionary time, a protest against a dying world, and it announces a new one."[5]   The *cri de coeur* most often quoted, however, and one that seems to illuminate the art of Karel Appel both in this historical and in his current phase affirmed that "A painting is no longer a construction of colors and lines, but an animal, a night, a scream, a human being and one and indivisible."[6] It comes as no surprise to learn that Appel, and many of the other artists in the group were published poets as well as exhibiting painters.

The Cobra group's identification of human and animal presences, reinforced by the suggestion of snake deification in their sobriquet, dated back to a mythological cult in ancient Nordic folklore, and it was repeated in the coiled snake colophon which appeared regularly in Cobra publications. This totem marker provides another clue to the expressive power,

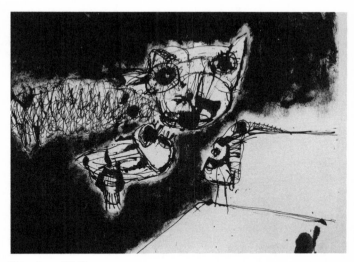

Drawing, 1949

and to the character of Karel Appel's art, both in his Cobra period and today, despite numerous significant changes that have occurred in other regards. His heaving landscapes, writhing clouds, and turbulent, primitivist animal imagery today tap a childhood vein whereby nature produces magical visions and betrays the viewer's deep primal instincts. Much like Dubuffet (but in a different fashion from the dadaists and surrealists who also influenced him at an early date), Appel set out in the beginning to repudiate all the elements of logic, analysis, and order that the School of Paris, as well as the French in their hedonistic way, and the dominant prewar constructivist tradition in a more puritanical mode seemed to prize above all.

Recently summarizing his sense of frustration with the leftover stylistic baggage of postwar European abstract Constructivist traditions, and his sense of urgency in addressing the task of inventing new forms to match his powerful feelings, Appel reflected on his early artistic odyssey and its many strands of inspiration:

"We were all looking for the real new image, fresh and new like a rebirth. We had to learn what came before—the Renaissance, Chinese art, the French art. The luminous feeling captured in Rembrandt's paintings touch the secret of life. Although Van Gogh's canvases are strong with joyous color, you experience in them the tragedy of life. Picasso was a major inspiration for me, also Matisse for color, and from the dadaist, Kurt Schwitters, I was infuenced to utilize found objects.

You have to learn it all; then forget it and start again like a child. This is the inner evolution. I speak about it all the time; it is the hardest thing for an artist."[7]

Among the many talented members of Cobra, Appel's great achievement was to bring together the naive but credible vision of the child with rather powerful and communicable feelings reflecting on the current condition of man in the postwar world, a world that had lost confidence in the more complex, rational and analytical views of art. Yet he was far from being a naive visionary, despite his simplistic forms and scintillating color. His work of this period establishes connections to that of de Kooning in the effort to grapple with both serious pictorial problems in an original inventive manner, and with current social and psychic tensions, ranging in their pictorial effects from desperation to tenderness, from absurdity to delectation. Appel's early art resembled, too, the horrifying changes that Picasso was working on the human anatomy at the time, reducing it to the ignominy of a visibly eroding humanity, in his grotesque repertory of figural images with their skewed features and redistributed body parts. Appel forced upon us a highly personal confrontation between dignity and distress, between contemporary man—the sublime ape—and the predatory beast lurking within him as his metaphor for dehumanization in the time following the most destructive world war and the profound indignities and oppression of the occupation.

Today Appel's imagery has lost none of its bite, or the acerbic challenge to our smug acceptance of the world as it is; his passion remains intact and undimmed. Over the past decade his painting has continued to evolve through a series of fascinating and unforeseen mutations, contained by a creative rhythm that was firmly established in its earliest creative phases. Appel left Holland for Paris in 1949 after Amsterdam officials, yielding to virulent press attacks on a mural commission for the city hall, closed it off from the public (it was reopened with considerable fanfare a decade later, as Appel's international reputation began to soar). Beginning in 1957, Appel divided his residence and painting activities between France and the United States, even as he does today, after experiencing on a New York visit the powerful and influential energies of the city and its Abstract Expressionist avant-garde. He quickly made their acquaintance in the now defunct Cedar Bar at University Place and Tenth Street. There he frequently consorted and conversed with de Kooning, Kline, and other painters. At the nearby Five Spot, below Astor Place, he also often shared libations with David Smith and experienced the nightly pleasures of Thelonious Monk's unflagging piano inventions. New York and its legendary postwar avant-garde helped liberate Appel, by his own account, from European pictorial inhibitions, introducing him to a new dynamism in art and life. His fresh vision of art came as a kind of epiphany that he can still recreate vividly in conversation, in his own pungent, personal idiom:

> When I came in 1957 to the United States, I saw in New York the unfinished space, you know, the buildings breaking down, and building up. And one day I was walking there and thinking, yes, there is no finished space here. Finish don't exist. Maybe only in small countries. I lived always in small finished countries like Holland, and it was good. But here there was unfinished space. Here I had also to *paint*

my paintings unfinished. Before I always feel I have to finish my paintings, but here not. I paint spontaneously like the jazz musicians, like the great orchestras of Count Bassie and Dizzy Gillespie, so wild. And the background of the painting here, in de Kooning and Kline, was so beautiful, too, even without paint on it. So, when I come to the United States, I find the unfinished space belongs to the painting *and becomes*, even without having to put paint on the canvas background. And that was my discovery in New York. And that's why I paint, first, not abstract, but "Action" painting; very direct spontaneous painting, and we keep it that way, not thinking, "Oh, I have to finish this part, and that part." No, the unfinished part belongs to art, and it belongs to the city, too. That is part of the beauty of the city. I find it in the States, in New York especially, that feeling. It is absolutely true. The traffic in the streets is without end. It is there, it is here, you cannot say, "Here it stops."

The new and absolutely vitalizing standards of completeness Appel discovered in American art, and life, have in recent years encouraged a bold and variable series of thematic and pictorial preoccupations ranging from humanistic concerns, almost cozily expressed in a personal kind of genre painting, to epic allegory and moods of apocalyptic violence. In paintings of 1979, shown the following year in Paris, Appel found himself in a new, more disciplined style of controlled, heavily emphatic and patterned brushstroke paintings, stressing lucidity and coherence—and rather homely themes. Landscape, trees, and such generic incidents as a woman wheeling a baby

Dizzy Gillespie with his portrait, New York, 1957.

Double Portrait of Harriet, 1980, 72 × 60″, oil on canvas

carriage on the New York streets attended by a comical dog were among their subjects. The painted surfaces were built up of large, uniform brushstrokes that changed direction, sometimes circling freely, sometimes set more tightly against one another in herringbone fashion. Patterns of uniform constructional elements, from which each form was built up, gave these sturdy brushstroke paintings a comforting equanimity and suggested that the painter wished to have his subject, technique, and emotions firmly in hand. *Double Portrait of Harriet*, a rather grave image of his longtime companion, Harriet De Visse, is an excellent example of this control. Yet his paintings are filled with warmth and good humor in this stabilizing phase of his art. Commenting on the work, the artist averred it had been inspired by the visible brushstrokes of his countryman Van Gogh, but in place of that artist's intensities and disequilibrium Appel substituted in his work the appeal of what he termed "the old sentiment of art." These humanistic qualities, inseparable in his mind from the artistic processes and its material evidence, he found most evident in artists as diverse as Van Gogh, Bonnard, Picasso and de Kooning. De Kooning's "angry women," he said, fused grimace and gesture, paint and pain. "His sentiment and feeling are in the brushstroke, not in illustration," noted Appel. "I tried to put back into painting of today what is missing, a certain sentiment of life and for the human being that has always been present in great art."

The evident formal constraints this mode of expression imposed on Appel soon gave way to broader pictorial effects and altogether more somber themes, when the artist returned to his New York studio from the placid and luxurious setting of his summer home in Monaco. Three he embarked on a rather brutal, if still stylized, series of "Crime" paintings. These are among Appel's most bizarre and sensational paintings, although their stiff Picassoesque mannerisms do something to take the edge off of their menace. Heavily outlined, schematized butcher knives are brandished in the air, a woman is brutally stabbed or sexually assaulted. A butcher walks in the street with a bleeding carcass on his shoulder; a cat mangles a bird. A monumental abstract work is created in six parts with mysterious signs in blue paint resembling body parts floating in a sea of black. The last gesture in the "Crimes" series is the most radical: a head is hunted in a chilling close-up of predatory, cannibalistic faces. Appel commented with helpless empathy on the shock of returning to the brutal realities of New York City after a summer on the luxuriously unreal and hedonistic French Côte d'Azur: "I feel the violence, the emotion in the city, the wildness of the dreadful pounding heart, I react, I feel I belong there."

Karel Appel's imagery today has lost none of its potency or bite although his personages seem less haunted, possessed or aggrieved. The consuming ferocity of the figure is unappeased in the Napoleonic prototype of *He Conquered the World*, but the sense of evil triumphant shrinks to a hollow grimace, subverted by the memento mori death's head that is set like a blazon on the hero's shield. In other emblematic portraits of this kind, the voluptuous and vibrant paint, so assuredly applied, remains fresh and incorruptible, persuading the viewer by its own particular kind of nervous truth and affirming the artist's authenticity by keeping facile, formulaic resolutions at bay. Here and there evidence of a profound, almost serene acceptance of the world and mankind reigns, despite their manifest foibles. Magical cloudscapes and prodigiously wrought heroic landscape designed for a new race of clumsy-footed yet affecting giants appear before us in a kind of mirage. We are transported by the vision; we cease to doubt romantic myth for a transient moment as we enter and approve Appel's visionary realm. Thus does the illusion of art reaffirm a coherent universe and human meaningful purposes.

There are also marked technical changes in Appel's work today, following the practices of his Cobra years when he tended to band and thus confine his forms with heavy black outlines. Colors now has a vivid life, freedom, and potency of its own, establishing a new theater of action; color also generates form and subject matter, liberated from drawing and connecting his forceful expression once again to de Kooning, whose facile but also unexpected play with medium keeps restating the theme of the eternal feminine, sometimes awkwardly, sometimes graciously, but always with the power of a worthy obsession. In describing the change in his art from symbol to sign to inspired mark in paint Appel has said: "Earlier my canvas was a virtual war, a body in a duel with paint. . [and] red was clearly blood. With my atomic war finally over, red is space. At that time [in the Cobra period] to build up a painting was the most fantastic feeling: little by little I have gone over to a magic space feeling."[8]

Despite his increasing mastery of abstraction and the magical, unfinished space of a New World esthetic, Appel remains today an instinctive allegorist. His dominant themes carry a strong charge of personal symbolism, distilled from a rich and massive life experience. The brilliant windmill series, which range in character from fugitive chimeras that are broken off from the earth and set luminously adrift in space in the clouds, to stolid, opaque terra-cotta constructions are, for him, representations of the human condition, polarized into masculine aspiration and a test of artistic will. Appel insists that the windmills have nothing to do with the landscape of his native Holland, but reaffirm the dilemma of man rooted to place but moving on currents of air in a space that symbolizes freedom and escape. The eternal human fugue from flesh and locale to spirit and emancipation are the true subject of these deceptively simplistic forms. Of them, he says:

The windmills I make have nothing to do with

Holland. You can find them everywhere. For me, they are human representations. It means we are born on this spot, and we stay on the earth, with our two feet on the ground, but we have still in our head the drive to freedom, and to new inventions. That is why the windmills turn around in space. Space is freedom.

He notes that he also enjoyed the risk and challenge of taking on such a kitsch subject, which could easily be mistaken for a reference to his country origin, a motif long since "degraded to a tourist postcard." To convert such dross into the refined and rare metal of artistic vision and human aspiration also restates his attraction to populist imagery, renewed in his urban street scenes. Appel is pleased to acknowledge his deep-rootedness in the world of everyday reality and the popular imagination, using it as a reproach to the pretensions and vacancy concealed under the rubric of educated high culture.

Appel's recent monumental paintings of nudes, supported by an exhaustive series of drawings also in heroic scale, carry for him a special significance that is not immediately apparent in the imagery. On one level they represent the age-old, idyllic dream of the female form reposing in a landscape, often merging its identity with the seductive, or alternately harsh, structures of the natural topography. But Woman in her psyche and mythos is his larger theme, a symbol of the natural rhythm of male passion, fulfillment, loss, and renewal, and also associated with the muse of creation and inspiration. She represents male longing and conflicted desire for passionate consummation, and the detached dream of peace and transquility. Interestingly, in 1957 Appel called his first obsessive investigation of the female forms his "tragic nudes" series. Reflecting on his high regard for Picasso's unquenchable, male's *volupté* and sensual invention in dealing with the female form, Appel has said, with evident sincerity, if perhaps an antiquated view of gender difference:

> The artist's life is based on nudes, on Woman. Every artist's life is dominated by that sentiment. All artists paint women and are dominated by women: Modigliani, Picasso, Matisse, and myself. Look at de Kooning. It is strange how male artists are obsessed with women. Even when we don't want it, we are still inspired and dominated by that feeling. It is unbelievable. The woman sometimes may want to be a windmill, like the man, but she stays a woman. That, for me, is the tragic side of the woman.

Some of the most gripping new work that has come from the hand of Appel is even more ambitious in aim and allegorical inference, dilating once again, as he has so often done in the past, on the man's hopes and fears. Grand

and masterful in scale, these recent paintings restate his desideratum of human sentiment, but in the context of catastrophic events and intimations of disaster. His repeated cloud paintings, in their leaden sobriety, turn our minds to Hiroshima, if not Chernobyl. He has also painted a number of politically oriented and truly macabre works, among them *Running Through* (1983, depicting Pope John Paul II's ghoulish visit to Auschwitz, his path beset by energetically mocking skulls of the lost dead. Appel's current agenda of cataclysm and deprivation defeats a contending impulse, in his later years, to seek a new vision of reconciliation, a Brave New World following the trials and social cruelties of the politics of destruction. The vision is flawed, however, and we have not yet approached Shakespeare's halcyon mood in *The Tempest*, for the protagonists more closely mimic Caliban than Ariel. Yet the characters, scenery, and mood are wonderfully piquent and moving. Some of his most ambitious, large scale works today affect an even more forbidding, stricken prescence with their resounding biblical themes and titles: *The Fall*, and *The Deluge*, or the doomsday intimations in *Before the Catastrophe*. One does not soon forget such poignant images as *Person in a Rainy Landscape*, with its huddled, rudimentary humanoid form bent beneath a lashing storm of what are, after all, only rather seductive and reassuring slivers of bright paint, no more, no less.

Here is a demiallegory that hasn't made up its mind whether to persuade, as in an argument, or to dissemble, like art; whether to consort with pain and despair, or to yield to an irrepressible desire to affirm humane values in man's all too brief existence on earth. With a seeming will of its own, the painting cheerfully subverts its rather grim illusion to come down on the artist's side as an unexpected, purely creative affirmation, perhaps thereby attaining an even more honest and persuasive impact than by restating the gloomy and familiar miseries and visual cliches of man's solitary fate. In the end, no matter how dismaying the appearance of Appel's subject matter may be, his protagonists transcend their mortal plight and torment by reclaiming, and reconstituting, their meaning in the supreme power and sorcery of visual depiction itself.

In his last exhibition held at the close of the year in New York, Appel once again veered and tacked in his art, departing from his grandiose nature themes and dilations on man's aggrieved condition. He turned to the new themes and formats that first appeared during the summer of 1986 when he made a series of lively gouaches on urban subjects to illustrate a volume of poetry by Octavio Paz, *Nocturne de San Idefonso*. A more condensed imagery emerged in the final line drawing illustrations which were actually used in Paz's book, with clear allusions to life in the city, a familiar Appel preoccupation. Ultimately, these images were to be tested in the new medium and scale of large oil painting in his recent show. The exhibition built upon these flat, topographic schemes, juxtaposing three or four compact narrative panels with abrupt linear divisions, while separating emblematic signs and symbols resembling a deck of playing-card faces. The terse, suggestive caricatures functioned as inscriptive signs for a variety of meanings in associative interplay.

In this exhibition catalogue, Donald Kuspit focused on presumed images of death and importance in *The Ship of Fools*. While the interpretation was illuminating and had obvious substance in this instance, the reductive thesis otherwise seemed clearly inappropriate to many of Appel's more naive and cozy genre scenes. In any case, the show had enough persuasive symbols of a macabre and menacing character to give legitimacy to the reading. Appel's imagery, however, also generated a strong counterforce reaffirming his natural ebullience in a celebration of the life-force. The aggressive, anomalous Polaroid constructions in giant scale which he bravely added to the show made a startling contrast in artistic texture and mood, as we shall see, to the relatively sober message of the paintings.

In the conventional painting medium, Appel exhibited a dense potpourri of multiple images and actions set in roughly schematized grids, to order to structure the spontaneity and fragments of visual narrative. *The Prairie* sets off a powerful ideograph of a bull against a spiky tree on a city street under a snowfall with a silhouette of a monkey on a branch—a strangely illogical amalgam of creatures, climates, and environments. Animal and human figuration, nature and culture, the wilderness and the asphalt jungle play off against each other throughout the entire painting series with a surprisingly coherent and persuasive interaction, creating stereotypical image clusters that call up memories of Appel's pictorial history and undoubtedly resonate in our own lives. The eerie combinations of powerfully stamped out and segmented images, painted thickly in vivid Fauvist color on dark grounds, leave a deceptive impression of innocent delight in the rudimentary paint matter and in primitive story-telling pictographs. These simple-minded idylls retempered, however, by undertones of dark violence, conveyed by grinning skulls, bloody masks, and other images of aggression. The viewer carries away the sense that all is not well with our world.

The mood and temper of Appel's disjunctive collection of pictographs fluctuate between the playful, the ominous, and the absurd, and his familiar and disarming images, conceived as they are with a childlike directness, persuade us of the uncorrupted authenticity of his vision. For this particular genre the phrase "the jesting grotesque" comes to mind. it is a phrase Clement Greenberg borrowed from Ruskin to characterize Mikro's work in his monograph on that artist.

In this same exhibition Appel managed to shock and even scandalize some of his most loyal followers with a strange new theater of monumental construction and photomontage. He had cut out and pasted the largest Polaroids mechanical technology makes possible today of a group of starling subjects—female nudes sliced up in awkward anatomical fragments, mounted on plywood armatures and stitched together with coils of thick nautical cord. These glossy nudes sported composite painting/photograph masks in anomalous outsize magnification. The backs of the giant puppets revealed coal-black silhouettes overpainted in violent, streaky color with leering visages, and hung about with more tangle of rough cord, mimicking the peep-show poses visible on their fronts. The dissonant and uglified figures achieved a savage power worthy of Dubuffet's crudest painted portraiture of the forties, which equated his friends in the literary *haute monde* with the wild scribbles and grinning masks of pathological art or wall graffiti.

Appel's disturbing images amount to something more than macabre clowning or childlike scribbles in a primitivist spirit. He persists in reading allegorical and philosophical meanings for our time into his imagery, as they test the limits of polite and visual discourse even by contrast with his uninhibited pictorial past. He feels that current levels of voyeurism and prurience in the media, and rampant images of sexist exploitation, whether in sex magazines or busstop shelters, can be recycled and used to artistic advantage if we care to view ourselves with a little more philosophical distance and calm. Where others might see only blatant sexuality in his imagery, or further evidence of the carnal/scapegoat female idol of psychology textbooks, he envisions a positive force. He has created a female sexual warrior allied to, and much enhanced by, modern technology (symbolized by his use of the slick, large-scale contemporary Polaroid). Many may experience distaste for the painful trusses and evil bindings which connect his sliced-up photo images of wild and grimacing female furies, and shrink from the cruel joke of the reverse image of their savage doppelgangers. Appel finds instead a symbolic unity of ego and id, savage and civilized discourse, the raw and the cooked in their presence.

Beyond that, in conversation he freely invents intriguing post-facto morality tales around these disjointed and unseductive nudes. He insists on reading their patched-up condition and vital if makeshift assemblage construction as a dramatic graph of progress from vulnerability and disreputability to regeneration. The figures signify for him the triumph of the maiden over a kind of commercial/technological anesthesia, or death by stupefaction from excessive visual ingestion of

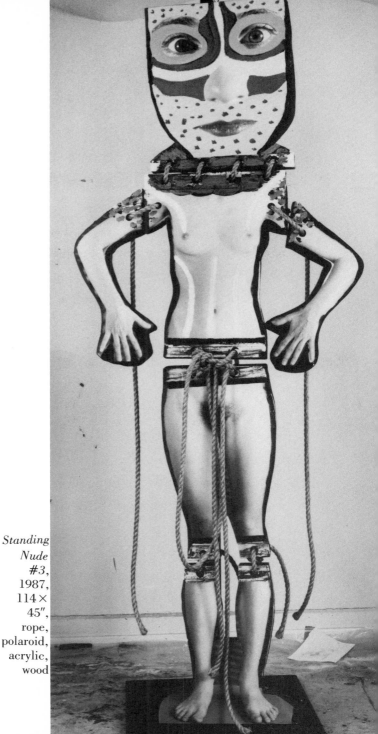

Standing Nude #3, 1987, 114 × 45″, rope, polaroid, acrylic, wood

the media and glossy four-color reproduction. Ironically, Walter Benjamin's argument of the loss of the sacred "aura" of the original work of art in the age of the mechanical reproduction is here turned against itself. Appel, a preeminent postwar expressionist, has, in fact, fallen in love with the mechanical image and the four-color process, and he has reclaimed an admittedly edited, glossy color photograph as a symbol of female rage rather than seductive acquiescence. In his chopped-up and reconstituted raving maenads he intends a positive image of the female survivor, and, undoubtedly, a sign of his own faith in the conditions of modern technological existence, for which his hypnotic, outsize Polaroid prints stand as a fetish/symbol.

Increasingly philosophical at the ripe and vigorous age of sixty-five, in the face of the sometimes unexpected but always edifying and tonic shifts in his art, ranging from the macabre in mood to the heroic and celebratory, Karel Appel never loses sight of his place in the history of art, nor of its vital lessons of change, renewal, and fresh hope:

> Behind painting is the mind. While I paint many different images, for me the important thing is always to go on in our Western Civilization, to go on with the

real evolution of art, so that we do not say, "Today is the end of our culture of art." No, we can always find a new truth there, so that we can then move ahead, each in his own way.

Man and Horse II, 1983, acrylic on paper, collage, 30¾ × 43"

NOTES

1. Michael Greenwood, "Appel: The Romantic Endures," *Arts of Canada*, December 1972, p. 56. Unless otherwise indicated, all the artist's remarks were made in conversation with the author in studio meetings in the spring and sumer of 1986, either in New York or Monaco.

2. Karel Appel, "C'est notre désir qui fait la revolution," *Cobra* no. 4, January 1, 1949. Published in Amsterdam, p. 3. Cited in Eleanor Flomenhaft, *The Roots and Development of Cobra Art* (Hempstead, New York, Fine Arts Museum of Long Island, 1985), p. 19.

3. Ibid., p. 27.

4. Alfred Frankenstein, *Karel Appel* (New York, Harry N. Abrams, Inc., 1979) p. 23.

5. Ibid., cited in Flomenhaft, p. 39.

6. Ibid., Flomenhaft, p. 39.

7. Eleanor Flomanhaft, interview with Karel Appel, October 1975, New York; cited in Flomenhaft, *The Roots and Development of Cobra Art*, Fine Arts Museum of Long Island, Hempstead, New York, 1986.

8. *Appel's Appels*, Rothmans of Pall Mall, Canada, Ltd. Exhibition catalogue, April 1972-July 1973; interview by Alan Hanlon, p. 18.

Nude, 1985, 5′ × 8′4″, acrylic, oilstick

CLOUDS, WINDMILLS, NUDES AND OTHER MYTHOLOGIES
by Sam Hunter

*I have learned over the years how to put oil paint on
canvas. Now I can do everything I want with paint. But it
is still a battle, it is still a struggle. At the moment, I am
still in the chaos. But for me, it is my character to make the
chaos positive. Today that is the spirit of our time. We live
always a tremendous chaos, and who can make the chaos
positive anymore? Only the artist.*

Karel Appel, Monaco 1986.

Mural, Stedelijk Museum, Amsterdam, 1951

Although he now enjoys a relatively serene, even magisterial, artistic maturity, over which he presides with resolute vigor and unflagging discipline, Karel Appel can look back in a spirit of sympathetic understanding to his early period of youthful rebellion as a budding Cobra master in the late forties. At that time he seemed compelled to use his art as a weapon, to shape and purge a postwar society still unable to fully comprehend, or disentangle itself from, the horrors of the war and the subsequent atmosphere of demeaning violence in the cold war aftermath. Making few distinctions between victor and vanquished, but appealing to our sense of outrage for the victims of all crimes against humanity, Appel created a new and gripping imagery of fantasy, heightening it with an incendiary pictorial violence of handling. These qualities helped establish the validity and essential thrust of the first important postwar European movement in art, Cobra, giving fresh contemporary relevance to the historical Expressionist experience.

For Appel, however, the war and its devastating aftermath in Holland, when he "prowled" the Dutch countryside—barely surviving—exchanging paintings "for a handful of potatoes, a bit of raw herring, or a couple of slices of sausage," provided both a platform for humanist sentiment and a reaffirmation, at the same time, of an ideal of creative transcendence. This unique synthesis of the allegorical with the creative impulse has persisted as perhaps the most important trait of his art. The critic Michael Greenwood stated the case eloquently for Appel's resolution of powerful and contending humanist and artistic inclinations when he wrote:

> "Appel's paintings, like those of Delacroix, express thematically and dynamically the state of conflict that is resolved in the act of creation. The artist's role, as he conceives it, is to fight his way back to a state of grace and in so doing offers mankind an exemplary model of reconciliation with the hidden forces of nature."[1]

Cobra became synonymous with a powerful expressionist current in art, embracing both figurative and abstract tendencies, which began to transform and reinvigorate European painting soon after the abrupt decline of the school of Paris, following the long, bleak years of the Nazi occupation. The movement received its name and character from a series of little-remembered but inter-related artistic developments in a remarkable collective efflorescence of creativity centered in three major European art centers; its name is made up of the first letters of the cities from which the artists came—Copenhagen, Brussels, and Amsterdam. As Europeans assimilated and then heroically liberated themselves from their physical and spiritual condition of wartime oppression, they conceived a new and vital interest in the human image, reflecting an awareness as never before of the fragility and contingency of human existence, a condition exacerbated by the terrors of the war and man's miraculous will to endure even under the most trying circumstances. Compared with the mythological regressions and flirtation with tragic content in American vanguard painting in the years between 1940 and 1948, dominated by the surrealizing tendencies of Pollock, Rothko, and others, postwar European art evinced a more unrelievedly somber character.

While this is not the appropriate moment to recapitualte in detail the history of the Cobra group, with its powerful expression and deep urge to return to roots and mythlogy, it has become increasingly clear (especially as the New York School has been subjected recently to an almost microscopically detailed reexamination) that, simply as a historical phenomenon, Cobra's wild and cathartic expressionist outburst commanded the passionate allegiance of artists throughout Europe and constituted an important new enthusiasm and historical episode. The Cobra years have their usefulness, too, as a prediction and model for the current neo-expressionist resurgence in Germany and Italy, different though the motives, mythic concerns, and individual accents may be in the two groups.

In one of the many pointed and laconic statements that have come down from this interesting postwar period, Karel Appel has given us his personal version of "the tradition of the new," with its special European resonance and unique cultural configuration: "To paint is to destroy what preceded it."[2] This important artistic Dutch pioneer was, of course, a founding member, with the Danish painter Asger Jorn and the Belgian poet Christian Dotremont, of Cobra. He was also mainly responsible for bringing the emerging expressionist avant-garde in Holland into contact with Danish and Belgian counterparts.

At the time he made his statement, in 1948, Appel had not yet arrived at his familiar and lavish painterly style, but was experimenting with rather stiff painted constructions reminiscent of the style of Schwitters, whose postwar exhibitions in Amsterdam deeply impressed him. Appel was instead creating *objets poubelles* (rubbish objects), physically related to, but spiritually quite at cross purposes from, the junk culture of the sixties and the encased, plasticized trash yet to be invented by Arman and the New Realists. Appel's depicted junk and found objects usually centered on a far more poignant and expressionist theme. In the construction the *Questioning children*, 1949, effigies of children of a Klee-like naïveté, and also reminiscent of the American Indian kachina figures Max Ernst came to admire and collect during World War II, were stacked up in brightly painted wood blocks nailed to a board; they seemed to confront a brutalized and hypocritical adult audience with the tragic waste of innocent lives, whether by force of arms or other means of oppression devised by a cruel and unrelenting society bent on self-destruction. Only one year later, in his *Child With Birds* (1950), the first of a number of Appel paintings to enter the collection of The Museum of Modern Art, New York, the artist had broken away from the perhaps strained social critique and poignancy of his construction phase to achieve a more individualized and complex scenario, depicting an equally affecting creatural world of predatory aggressors and their prey. Somewhat reminiscent of Picasso, these first mature Cobra works had an entirely individual vision in their strangely exhilarating combination of vivid primary color, thick impasto, and virulent subject matter bordering on the grotesque. At the same time, primitivist expression was fused significantly with a loaded brushstroke and gestural abstraction.

Karel Appel's imagery today has lost none of its potency or bite, although his personages seem less haunted, possessed, or aggrieved. The consuming ferocity of the figure is unappeased in the Napoleonic prototype *He Conquered the World*, but the sense of evil triumphant shrinks to a hollow grimace, subverted by the *memento mori* death's head set like a blazon on the hero's shield. In other emblematic portraits of this kind, the voluptuous and vibrant paint, so assuredly applied, remains fresh and incorruptible, persuading the viewer by its own particular kind of nervous truth and affirming the artist's authenticity by keeping

Titan Series #2, 1988 77 × 66″, mirror, rope, polaroid, acrylic on wood

facile, formulaic resolutions at bay. Here and there evidence of a profound, almost serene, acceptance of the world and mankind reigns, despite their manifest foibles. Magical cloudscapes and prodigiously wrought heroic landscapes designed for a new race of clumsy-footed yet affecting giants appear before us in a kind of mirage. We are transported by the vision; we cease to doubt romantic myth, for a transient moment, as we enter and approve Appel's visionary realm. Thus does the illusion of art reaffirm a coherent universe and meaningful human purposes.

There are also marked technical changes in Appel's work today, following the practices of his Cobra years, when he tended to band and thus to confine his forms with heavy black outlines. Color now has a vivid lie, a freedom and potency of its own, establishing a new theater of action; color also generates form and subject matter, liberated from drawing and connecting his forceful expression once again to De Kooning, whose facile but also unexpected play with medium keeps restating the theme of the eternal feminine—sometimes awkwardly, sometimes graciously, but always with the power of a worthy obsession. In describing the change in his art form symbol to sign to inspired mark in paint, Appel has said, "Earlier my canvas was a virtual war, a body in a duel with paint. . . [and] red was clearly blood. With my atomic war finally over, red is space. At that time [in the Cobra period] to build up a painting was the most fantastic feeling: little by little I have gone over to a magic space feeling."[3]

Despite his increasing mastery of abstraction and the magical "unfinished" space of a New World esthetic, Appel remains today an instinctive allegorist. He dominant themes carry a strong charge of personal symbolism, distilled from a rich and massive life experience. The brilliant "windmill" series, which ranges in character from fugitive chimeras, broken off from the earth and set luminously adrift in space in the clouds, to stolid opaque terracotta constructions, represents, for him, the human condition, polarized into masculine aspiration and a test of artistic will. Appel insists that the windmills have nothing to do with the landscape of his native Holland, but reaffirm the dilemma of man rooted to place but moving on currents of air in a space that symbolizes freedom and escape. The eternal human fugue from flesh and locale to spirit and emancipation is the true subject of these deceptively simplistic forms. He says,

> "The windmills I make have nothing to do with Holland. You can find them everywhere. For me, they are human representations. It means we are born on this spot, and we stay on the earth, with our two feet on the ground, but we have still in our head the drive to freedom, and to new inventions. That is why the windmills turn around in space. Space is freedom."

He notes that he also enjoyed the risk and challenge of taking on such a kitsch subject, which could easily be mistaken for a reference to his country of origin, a motif long since "degraded to a tourist postcard." To convert such dross into the refined and rare metal of artistic vision and human aspiration also re-states his attraction to populist in the world of everyday reality and the popular imagination, using it as a reproach to the pretensions and vacancy (which Dubuffet was the first to campaign against) concealed under the rubric of educated high culture.

Appel's recent monumental paintings of nudes, supported by an exhaustive series of drawings also in heroic scale, carry for him a special significance not immediately apparent in the imagery. On one level they represent the age-old, idyllic dream of the female form reposing in a landscape, often merging its identity with the seductive, or alternately harsh, structures of the natural topography. But woman in her psyche and mythos is his larger theme, a symbol of the natural rhythm of male passion, fulfillment, loss, and renewal, and also associated with the muse of creation and inspiration. She represents male longing and conflicted desire for passionate consummation, and the detached dream of peace and tranquility. Interestingly, Appel in 1957 called his first obsessive investigation of female form his "tragic nudes" series. Reflecting on his high regard for Picasso's unquenchable male *volupté* and sensual invention in dealing with the female form, Appel has said with evident sincerity (if perhaps an antiquated view of gender difference):

> *"The artist's life is based on nudes, on woman. Every artist's life is dominated by that sentiment. All artists paint women and are dominated by women: Modigliani, Picasso, Matisse, and myself. Look at De Kooning. It is strange how male artists are obsessed with women. Even when we don't want it, we·are still inspired and dominated by that feeling. It is unbelievable. The woman sometimes may want to be a windmill, like the man, but she stays a woman. That, for me, is the tragic side of the woman."*

The most gripping new work has come from the hand of Appel is even more ambitious in aim and allegorical inference, dilating once again, as it has so often done in the past, on

Running Through, 1983, two panels, 6 × 16', oil on canvas

man's hopes and fears. Grand and masterful in scale, the new paintings restate his desideratum of human "sentiment," but in the context of catastrophic events and intimations of disaster. His repeated cloud paintings, in their leaden sobriety, turn our minds to Hiroshima, if not Chernobyl. Appel has also painted a number of politically oriented and truly macabre works, among them *Running Through* (1983), depicting Pope John Paul II's ghoulish visit to Auschwitz, his path beset by energetically mocking skulls of the lost dead. Appel's current agenda of catacysm and deprivation defeats a contending impulse, in his later years, to seek a new vision of reconciliation, a Brave New World following the trials and social cruelties of the politics of destruction. The vision is flawed, however, and we have not yet approached Shakespeare's halcyon mood in *The Tempest*, for the protagonists more closely mimic Caliban than Ariel. Yet the characters, scenery, and mood are wonderfully piquant and moving. Some of Appel's most ambitious, large-scale works today effect an even more forbidding, stricken presence, with their resounding biblical themes and titles: *The Fall, The Deluge*, or the doomsday intimations in *Before the Catastrophe*. One does not soon forget

Long Shall They Live, detail, 1987, 76 × 96″, oil on canvas such poignant images as *Person in a Rainy Landscape*, with its huddled, rudimentary humanoid form bent beneath a lashing storm of what are, after all, only rather seductive and reassuring slivers of bright paint, no more, no less.

Here is a demi-allegory that seemingly hasn't made up its mind whether to persuade, as in an argument, or to dissemble, like art; whether to consort with pain and despair or to yield to an irrepressible desire to affirm hman values in man's all-too-brief existence on earth. With a seeming will of its own, the painting cheerfuly subverts its rather grim illusion to come down on the artist's side as an unexpected, purely creative affirmation, perhaps thereby attaining an even more honest and persuasive impact than by restating the gloomy and faimiliar miseries and visual clichés of man's solitary fate. In the end, no matter how dismaying the appearance of Appel's subject matter may be, his protagonists transcend their mortal plight and torment by reclaiming, and reconstituting, their meaning in the supreme power and sorcery of visual depiction itself.

Increasingly philosophical at a ripe and vigorous age of sixty-five, in the face of the sometimes unexpected but always edifying and tonic shifts in his art, ranging from the macabre to the heroic and celebratory, Karel Appel never loses sight of his place in the history of art, nor of its vital lessons of change, renewal, and fresh hope:

> *"Behind painting is the mind. While I paint many different images, for me the important thing is always to go on in our western civilization, to go on with the real evolution of art, so that we do not say, "Today is the end of our culture of art." No, we can always find a new truth there, so that we can then move ahead, each in his own way."* (from catalogue of exhibition at Museum of Art, Fort Lauderdale, Florida 1986).

NOTES

1. Michael Greenwood, "Appel: The Romantic Endures," *Arts of Canada*, December 1972, p. 56. Unless otherwise indicated all the artist's remarks were made in conversation with the author in studio meetings in the spring and summer of 1986, either in New York or Monaco.

2. Karel Appel, 'C'est notre désir qui fait la révolution," Cobra (Amsterdam), no. 4 (January 1, 1949), p. 3. Cited in Eleanor Flomenhaft, *The Roots and Development of Cobra Art*, Fine Arts Museum of Long Island, Hempstead (New York) 1985, p. 19.

3. *Appel's Appels*, exhibition catalogue, Rothman's of Pall Mall, Canada, April 21, 1972-July 9, 1973; interview by Alan Hanlon, p. 18.

STREET ART AT THE VILLA
EL SALVADOR
Karel Appel and his Friends

1979

El Salvador is a slum town in the Peruvian desert where, in 1976, Karel Appel created a series of murals with the Indians.

26 A slum outside Lima, Peru. Nothing but sand, dry sand and burning sun... A desert silence broken only by the sound of a single loudspeaker.

58 A self-made town, an honest community, named with a brave optimism: Villa El Salvador, the City of the Savior.

94 It is in this rough but hope-filled place that Karel Appel, the Dutch painter who has made the world his home, has made new friends. One of his companions is affectionately filming the project, the creation of "street art" on the walls of the local bank.

134 Street art is a group art—it impacts upon the community as a whole. It unites the bank director...

149 The building painter, the neighborhood plumber... and the mayor's wife.

161 Mural painting is different from all

other types of art. It is linked organically to the architecture, to people's everyday living space.

174 Appel says that "painting is a living substance, a spiritual light, a sincere warmth. It's probably the most social means of expression because it is visible by all, everyone has access to it. It responds to the social traits inherent in every human being, for everyone is creative.

217 For street art to blossom in El Salvador, Appel must touch the community spirit. During the work a contact develops that unites everyone creating the murals, a concept of art that motivates us to go on painting and prevents us from descending to mechanical reproduction.

277 It is a moving energy, a "warm" dimension. The infinite gives birth to the finite.

295 Every day at noon a shop becomes a restaurant in which the jovial proprietor cooks for the artists. Appel doesn't speak Spanish very well, but art creates solid links. His collaborators become his friends.

325   However, the harsh reality of their surroundings is never far off. Violent sand storms often come up, blinding the unprepared. It never rains in this corner of Peru.

357   Yet here is where the inhabitants of El Salvador decided to accept hardships and conquer them.

372   "Color is the stimulant that helps us attain ecstasy, to give more of ourselves," Appel says. In evoking that pure joy Appel attempts to touch something that lies even deeper than human thought. He breaks the pitiless white light down into colors, and color into elementary shapes and basic elements.

428   The town undergoes a dizzying metamorphosis, the fresco dances across the bank's wall. . . and reality turns into magic.

479   Children take over with tumultuous energy. While drawing and color jostle each other, a dialogue begins between thought and mind, nature and culture.

496   This painting and its free association seem to provoke an instinctive and immediately felt happiness. The

intoxication the shapes create is partly due to their gay colors, to the inventive composition and the astonishingly dimensional rendering. . .

512   This feeling of exuberance also comes from spontaneity, from authenticity, from seeming insouciance, from the impression that we are very close to the experience of creation.

612   Inevitably, everyone feels the desire to create—even someone in a bank. A major problem for art is the control of spontaneity and formality. Today, people sometimes give the impression that they cannot tell the difference between chaos and freedom, but freedom is not anarchy. Appel says that he always begins from a "positive chaos." In other words, he uses it as the starting point for creating something, something between chaos and order.

751   A warm and debonair atmosphere created by change in the environment. As the days go by, the community shows a growing interest in the painting. Work will go on after the

bank is open...

770 The work turns into an object of individual pride: our old friend, the painter installed.

814 The El Salvador art acquires a certain reputation. The Peruvian Minister of Education and Culture makes a special trip. She is impressed.

832 Another high official is not. "It's not art," he remarks contemptuously, "it's child's play." "Precisely," replies Appel, laughing. "We are trying to express the game-playing aspect of life."

859 There is still some paint left. What will be done with it? Appel consults with his artist friends...paint the cement tower that has become the town's symbol. They set to work with a new assurance...

903 ...and a daring mastery—an ease in painting a straight line, to take your breath away with a stroke.

920 Water barrels represent the only water source in this desert town, but that doesn't dishearten the people of El Salvador.

946 The townschildren have taken part in

something extraordinary; a shared vision and an artistic creation. . . street art, moved by a touching energy and contagious enthusiasm.

985   The children have made a new friend. . . a magician who has helped them discover an expression of beauty and solace.

1002   The street art project has taken ten days, and is declared a success. The smooth surface of the wall, the rhythm of form, colors and lines seem to come from the children.

1032   Appel often describes his experience in El Salvador as a kind of symphony.

1059   Art is a constant transformation of everyday things. At Villa El Salvador, it was also eloquent proof of man's spirituality.

Drawing, 1980

KAREL APPEL: NEW APPARITIONS
by Rupert Martin

1986

I'd really like to have the eye of an animal who'd taken it into its head to paint the human world.[1]

Rupert Martin

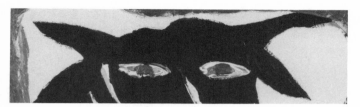

The Prairie (detail), 1986, 96 × 76″ on canvas.

1. The Eye of An Animal.

There is a restless energy in Karel Appel's paintings, a struggle to come to terms with the inchoate world, a desire to express the vitality of the human soul and the essence of ordinary things. Seeing is for him an essential key to the soul, a way of preserving the freshness of life in the face of stultifying routine. "It's difficult for us to get off the rails of routine. We stop seeing the world. Our gaze seems fixed, the world grinds to a halt. It's death closing in."[2] In order to live fully the eye must remain "alert like a radar,"[3] sensitive not only to the surface of things but to what lies beyond the surface. Appel believes that the movement of thought and feeling can be perceived and translated through dynamic forms of expression.

Drawing, 1980, ink on paper

"By kinetic thought I mean something very simple: the attempt to grasp movement in all its spontaneity, right in the middle of a living reality fertilized by the imagination. A painting, the very act of painting has to make the speed and the lie of this movement felt. Which is to say that it is more than an act of 'perception'! I'd rather talk of a leap that you take right into the native depth of things."[4]

What alerts the eye of an animal is movement. Similarly the eye of an artist such as Karel Appel is captivated by the shifting surfaces of life. Not only does the artist respond to the movement surrounding him, he has a role to play in animating things. "The function of artists. . . is to set things in motion again, so as to discover what is hidden, what is emergent."[5] The movement of a brushstroke can bring something that is dormant or latent of life. "In my painting I try to capture the movement that whirls perpetually in things and in the mind."[6] Paradoxically in Appel's painting, the creative urge can also be a destructive one. His painting is characterized by the energy with which he attacks the canvas. The primal instinct of an animal is savage, often destructive, and the analogy is one that Appel himself often uses.

"To paint is to destroy what preceded. I never try to make a painting, but a chunk of life. It is a scream; it is at night; it is like a child; it is a tiger behind bars."[7]

The very word Cobra (the group with which Appel was associated at the start of his artistic career) suggests the potent, sometimes destructive power of the animal world. The artists from Copenhagen, Brussels and Amsterdam who formed that group after World War II felt an urge to break away from the sophistications and the elegant academicism which they felt characterized the school of Paris. Their urge to destroy was a creative one.

> *"A few of us got together: Corneille, Alechinsky, Constant. With the big cataclysm behind us, we were full of revolt and tension. We needed a new form of expression, we needed it desperately, violently. We wanted to get to grips with painting, do something different. For that we had to destroy all we'd learned, get rid of all the culture accumulated through school and academy, even forget the very history of Europe! . . .But it was when I came across the self-destructive forms of Picasso that I got a real shock! They made me feel our whole civilization was in the process of blowing up."[8]*

What emerged was the intense burst of activity during the Cobra years of 1948-51, when the primitive urgency of Appel's paintings began to be recognized. In the first monograph on Karel Appel in 1962, Herbert Read referred to this connection with animal life:

> *"Such art is not classical, for it has no measure of containment, no sweetness or rest. It is the agitated art of the Gothic, of the North, which was always preoccupied with movement, with boundless space, with infinity. It was also preoccupied with animal vitality . . ."[9]*

Another aspect of the Cobra artists was the child-like simplicity of their forms and the inspiration they drew from children's paintings with their spontaneous, uninhibited splashes of bright color and their crude shapes. Karel Appel's series of three reliefs entitled *Questioning children* (1948) marks a crucial stage in the evolution of his style. The rough, irregular wooden surfaces, the primary colors and the bright quizzical expressions on the faces of the children, have the freshness and hope of a generation that has not had to live through the war. Not only did Appel find a new vitality in children's paintings, but he also recognized in their questioning faces his own perpetual questioning as an artist, his constant quest for new forms of expression, and his creative revolt against the established order of things and the tyranny of routine.

"When I stand back and take a look at my work, it seems to me that what I've been doing is to shout out my love of freedom. To say 'no' to the established order, that's the function of art."[10]

Gouache, 1985

2. New Apparitions

*"And when with my hand holding the paint and my
eyes seeing the form, I touch the canvas, it trembles, it
comes to life. The struggle begins to harmonize canvas,
eye, hand, forms. New apparitions stalk the earth."[11]*

After thirty years the spirit of Cobra still
pervades Appel's work but the forms are being
constantly renewed, his imagery transformed
by his vision of the world as it is, and by his
prophetic and apocalyptic vision of the world
as it is becoming. To leap from the years of
Cobra to the 1980s is to leap from the aftermath of one war to the threat of another. To
both situations Appel has responded in an
urgent, allusive but none the less relevant way.
The concern he shows, in his paintings of the
1980s, with poverty and oppression, crime and
the disintegration of our cities is partly inspired by his experience of living in New York,
where he moved in 1957.

Painted photograph, 1984

"When I've been back in New York for a week," he has said, *"the life of the city grabs me and I take no interest inlight any more, but I paint the 'crimes', that belong to the aggressiveness of the city."[12]*

The New York paintings express the violence, darkness and poverty of city life.

"I feel the violence, the emotion in the city, the wildness of the dreadful pounding heart, I react, I feel I belong there."[13]

The painting *Crime I*, 1980, is one of a series of paintings in which the horror of the scene is depicted in the violent tension of the brush-strokes, and where the dramatic stylization of the figures reflects the influence of Picasso's depiction of violence, in paintings such as *Guernica* and in the post-war painting *War*. In these paintings of Appel, the controlled meshes of tightly-knit brushstrokes, inspired by Van Gogh's technique of hatched strokes, reaches its ultimate expression. The patterns of short parallel brushstrokes characterizing Appel's paintings from 1974 give way around 1980 to a freer, more expressive use of line and a more organic rhythm. The paintings *Nude* (1980) and *Chair* (1980), reveal the transition very clearly. What develops is the concern with figurative form. The years of disciplined focussing on detail in his paintings of still-lifes, leads to a new humanist vision rich in incident and detail, but possessing a greater scope and intensity. The unbridled vigor of the Cobra years returns, as the artist discovers subjects of universal human interest, and begins to paint again in a visionary manner and on an epic scale.

Three paintings in particular reveal a concern with the plight of the down-and-out in *New York, Street Scene* (1981), *The Beggar* (1983), and *Winter in New York* (1983). The mask-like whiteness of the child's face in *Street Scene*, the haunted intensity of the mother's look, and the empty begging bowl, are painted with a passion that comes from a sense of pity and indignation. In *The Beggar*, the outstretched leg, the despairing face are painted with thick impasto against the backdrop of a burning building. Shelley's words "Hell is a city much like London" are true today of New York and other cities, in which not only is the human spirit crushed, but the fabric of the city itself also appears to be disintegrating. *Walking Through the Fallen City* (1982), expresses this sense of urban decay. The city appears as a tangled, fragmentary, transitory place in which human beings are trapped, and from which only the bird symbolically escapes. In *Black Clouds Over City* (1984),[14] the clouds hover ominously over the city that could represent either Old Amsterdam with its tall warehouses, or New Amsterdam (New York) with its skyscrapers. The elemental forces of nature seem to threaten the vulnerable city.

War and Hunger, originally entitled *Questioning*, is more explicit in its symbolism, connecting the prevalence of war and the spread of arms with the fact of hunger. This is perhaps Appel's most overtly polemical painting; a statement of compassion at a worldwide problem; an indictment of the expenditure on arms and their sale to Third World countries, which helps to create rather than to alleviate hunger. There is an almost prophetic warning in this fierce painting made in 1983, before the famine in Ethiopia assumed catastrophic dimensions, and the third panel of the triptych with its barren, desert landscape is a disturbing image of desolation. Equally disturbing, although more ambiguous, is the series of apocalyptic cloud paintings which follow in a cluster in 1984. In *Sky With Clouds I* and *Boat With Clouds*, the bright colors make the paintings appear more radiant and optimistic. Appel's enthusiasm is evident in a statement made in 1984:

> "Look, a clouded sky, like it's never been painted before in western culture. Van Gogh, Goya, no landscape painter has ever done it like that. Once again, it appeared completely out of the blue. I keep looking, thinking and when suddently it happens: Hey clouds! and what clouds![15]   "...And I go on probing. I'm always doing it. I've already painted ten large works like this. As you can see: red clouds green sky a woman in the sky. One of the three marvels of her life."[16]

The clouds have a visionary quality, appearing as a subject for Appel's painting out of his subconscious as well as his memory. They begin, like the birds in earlier paintings, as symbols of freedom, espressions of new forms, sculpted by the wind and unfurling like an apocalyptic scroll over a diminutive landscape, dotted with windmills, trees or houses.

By contrast with the dense jungle of his Cobra paintings or his recent city paintings, a sense of infinite space is created by the aerial perspective and the light. These skies recall the paintings of Nolde with their vivid orange, yellow or purple color, or the restless skies of Van Gogh's later paintings, swirling with lines of energy. One of the main differences is of scale. Appel's clouds are conjured up with immense swathes of paint applied with a mastery of handling that makes the surfaces tactile, luminous and full of motion. Combined with their overwhelming scale is their bright colour. In *Sky With Clouds I*, the clouds swirl over a yellow and green horizon, just as in *Boat With Clouds* the clouds with the ship hover over an orange horizon. The clouds consist of various colors, red, blue, green, black, shot through with streaks of turquoise and purple like lightning. The paint, mixed with egg tempera to give it luminosity and fluency, is applied wet on wet so that colors merge or are superimposed in layers. The subject of clouds is one that has obsessed northern painters such as Nolde and Munch, but Appel has added another dimension to this tradition. Within this tradition clouds often take a psychological role, reflecting the mood and anxiety of the

Painted photograph, 1984

artist or the mood of the scene depicted. The stylized whorl of clouds in Munch's *The Scream* reflects the anguish of the figure in the foreground isolated within the landscape. Appel's clouds have similar lines of energy, as well as possessing the saturated color of Nolde's luminous expanses of cloud, hovering over the flat landscape. They are alive with the electrical energy of a thunderstorm about to break, and are laden with foreboding; the colors seem almost radioactive in their lurid intensity. This might seem too literal a reading in the light of recent events, but several of these recent paintings have the hallucinatory character of a premonition. One painting, entitled *Before the Catastrophe* (1985), shows two warlike, almost mythological figures contending with the elements and creating chaos. Another painting, entitled *The Deluge* (1984), shows the aftermath of a catastrophe with the human forms in the foreground being swept away by the torrents pouring down from the sky and mountainsides.

Appel's New York paintings of the 1980s are characterized not only by a renewed energy and confidence but by a startling relevance to critical areas of concern and debate; crime, poverty, hunger, nuclear disaster and the threat of war. The paintings embody some of these areas of concern, but their strength lies in their direct, authentic vision of the world. Inspiration is the vital, motivating force in Appel's work, and can lead him to transcend the conscious mind:

"Look at the clouds on that canvas. A low horizon. Typical Dutch landscape painter. All the same I wasn't thinking of Holland when I painted it. Ce dépasse la nature. Ce dépasse ma jeunesse; ce dépasse toute ma vie. That's my work."[17]

As a counterpoint to some of his more threatening landscapes, there are also the visionary landscapes, such as *Floating Windmills*, 1984, which with its glowing colours, its sense of freedom, symbolized by the wind passing through the sails of the windmills, and its evocation of the past, conveys a warmth of feeling that derives from both memory and imagination. Appel's painting is so full of vitality that it would be misleading to present him as a harbinger of doom. The subjects in these works can be painful but they can be interpreted in positive as well as negative

Person in a Rainy Landscape, 1986, 72 × 96″, oil on canvas

ways, and the essential vision of these works is not pessimistic. There may be a tragic intensity, a reconciliation of opposites, a cry of anger, but it is this that shocks us into an awareness of all that we might lose; our humanity and hope. In the painting entitled *Encounter with God*, 1981, Appel portrays a meeting between man and God against an animated white background. The outstretched arms of the figure on the right imply an acceptance and reconciliation, far different from the loneliness and isolation of the figures depicted in the disintegrating cities of other recent paintings.

Another side of Appel's work can be seen in the calmer, lighter paintings made in the South of France where he spends the summer each year. In his series of window paintings the light of the South creates a more harmonious vision, a counterbalance to the fierceness of the New York paintings. The most recent painting in this exhibition was painted in the South and is called *La résurrection de la femme*, 1985. Beneath a tranquil sky between two outcrops of rock, a figure with outstretched hand hovers above the dormant body of a woman. The woman murdered in *Crime* is restored to life and dignity in a serene uncomplicated painting full of light and harmony.

3. An expression of my era

The atmosphere I inhale and make tangible by my paint is an expression of my era[11].
Karel Appel, 1950.

The new painting of Karel Appel in the 1980s coincides with resurgence of an expressionist style of painting which draws some of its inspiration from German Expressionism as well as from a reassessment of the importance of COBRA. It would be easy, but misleading to associate Appel's recent work with the work of the younger generation of European painters such as George Baselitz, A.R. Penck, Enzo Cucchi and Anselm Kiefer. Whilst there are certain similarities in the uninhibited handling of paint and the expressive use of line and color these are coincidences that are symptomatic of the anxious and turbulent Eighties. Several times in the past Appel has commented on the way in which artists can develop apparently similar styles and yet be ignorant of each other's work.

> "It wasn't until 1957, in New York, that I saw the revolutionary canvases that Pollock had painted during the war. They really were close to the spirit of Cobra, at least on the imaginative side. I also saw the work of De Kooning. It's not the first time that men of the same period, though widely apart, have shared the same mentality and arrived at the same conclusions. It's kind of reassuring!"[19]

Paradoxically Appel's expressionist style of painting derives from the Post-Impressionist work of Van Gogh, and not from German Expressionism. This is perhaps one of the crucial differences between Appel's recent paintings and those of his contemporaries. His concern is with the transforming alchemy of paint, transcending the material and creating an immaterial vision of light and form. A painter such as Anselm Kiefer depicts a more sombre, burnt landscape. Appel has himself commented on Kiefer's work:

> "There is a great sentiment, a great feeling in his painting. A sense of something smouldering, of something that is burnt out but is still smelling. A burnt out world where nothing grows."[20]

Kiefer's relationship with history is also radically different. Whereas Appel has survived and assimilated the World War and creates "a movement to the future," Kiefer is concerned to reconcile himself and his native culture to past from which he has been dislocated by the same war. His attempt to retrieve lost areas of Germany's history and mythological past, spuriously appropriated by the Nazi ideology, is a brave and heroic endeavour to build a new basis for painting in his country. Appel, by contrast, has always been something of an exile and a nomad, the influence of his native land coming more from its paintings than from its landscape or history. Whereas Kiefer's approach was born out of his conceptual works of the 1970s, and shows a sophisticated sense of irony, Appel's concern is with pure painting and with an innocence of vision which allows him to develop ideas in a spontaneous, painterly way. Herbert Read wrote that "Appel is not a conceptual artist, *un peintre raisonable*. His control of design is as instinctive as a child's."[21] Each artist provides us with an equally strong and valid vision for the 1980s, but the diffences between them are more revealing than any ostensible similarities in style.

Appel has spoken over a period of time about the satisfaction of pure painting. In 1950 he wrote:

> "*Painting is a tangible, sensual experiencing, intensely moved by joy and the tragedy of man. A spatial experiencing, fed by instinct becomes a living shape. The atmosphere I inhale and make tangible by my paint is an expression of my era.*"[22]

This is as true of his painting now as it was of his painting during the Cobra period. In 1976 he wrote:

> "*Painting is a living substance which transmits human warmth a spiritual glow, a genuine warmth. It is the most social means of expression, because it is visible to all and can be felt by everyone. It responds to the social traits inherent in each human being for everyone is creative.*"[23]

Painting for Karel Appel may be a very personal struggle, but it is also the "most social means of expression," a way of communicating fresh images of the familiar world or surprising visions of the unknown, and the new paintings of the 1980s provide an often disturbing but ultimately invigorating insight into the contradictions of the human soul.

NOTES

1. Interview with Frederick de Towarnicki, Paris, May 1977, published in Alfred Frankenstein: Karel Appel, Harry Abrams, New York, 1980, p. 157.

2. Ibid. p. 160.

3. Ibid. p. 158.

4. Ibid. p. 158.

5. Ibid. p. 160.

6. Ibid. p. 160.

7. Quoted in Hugo Claus: Karel Appel, A.J.G. Strengholt's Publishing Company, Amsterdam, 1962, p.63.

8. Interview with Frederick de Towarnicki, op.cit., p. 162.

9. Herbert Read in Hugo Claus; Karel Appel, op.cit., p. 8.

10. Interview with Frederick de Towarnicki, op.cit., p. 157.

11. Hugo Claus; Karel Appel, op.cit., p. 140-1.

12. Quoted in Wim Beeren: The New Work of Karel Appel, paintings 1979-1981, Museum Boymans-van Beuningen, Rotterdam, 1982, p. 4

13. Ibid. p. 20.

14. In "The New Reality of Karel Appel", *Dutch Art and Architecture Today*, no. 16, Eindhoven. December 1984, p. 4, Gijs van Tuyl writes: "In *Black Clouds over City*, he first made a painstakingly accurate painting of this exceptional form of veduta. He then painted it over "like a gust of wind", sweeping away the realistic view with shades of grey and black, leaving a few traces of green."

15. Interview with Ischa Meijer, *Vrij Nederland*, 28 April 1984. Quoted in Karel Appel, catalogue, Listasafr Islands. June 1984, p. 18.

16. Ibid. p. 18.

17. Ibid. p. 25.

18. Interview with Frederick Towarnicki, op.cit., p. 49.

19. Ibid. p. 165.

20. Quoted in Rasaad Jamie: "Appel Now". *Artscribe*, no. 45, February-April 1984, p. 43.

APPEL NOW
by Rasaad Jamie

1984

Drawing, 1980

In the London gallery where I met Karel Appel for this interview were a number of recent paintings which didn't look like his work—notably, a painting of a window, in 1980. Its meditativeness, geometry and ordered brushstrokes were directly contrary to what one conceives of as the qualities of his work. Viewing this painting is as disorienting as meeting the artist. One is surprised to find that he is getting on. It indicates the extent to which one's conception of Appel is fused with certain of his paintings: the idea of eternal youth, of exuberance, of a madcap fervor, at once virile and childlike.

Today one's perception of Appel is inevitably mediated by the after-image of a personality (in complete and absolute alignment with the power and vitality of the work) which was relentlessly presented between 1957 and 1965 when Appel gained and consolidated his reputation as a Euorpean painter of considerable force, when these seemed to be thin on the

Dizzy Gillespie with two of his portraits, Nice, 1969.

ground. It is an image of Appel as a sturdy, virile young artist: among his contemporaries he was by far the most sexual, the most charismatic figure. In one memorable photograph he crouches, paint-stained, in a studio filled with powerful, heavily impastoed paintings (the impression is that he paints like a bird sings). There is the 1961 documentary, *The Reality of Karel Appel*, in which, to the sounds of Dizzie Gillespie's *Lyric for Appel* (improvised while Appel painted Gillespie's portrait, taping the performance) he squirts paint at the canvas from outsize tubes or flings it on with a palette knife. "I in my uproar," was his cry at the time. In 1963, a huge, glossy, but perceptively written monograph appeared authored by Appel's friend, the Belgian poet/novelist Hugo Claus. Appel's paintings, he wrote, are "like a hot shriek which goes on, shimmering in the frozen air."

This image emerged out of, and was enforced by, the raw power and presence of Appel's paintings of the fifties. It could be argued that in relative terms, all Appel did was to neglect to retard or contradict the idea of the painter which his work of this time suggested so vividly and so compellingly: the idea that paintings of such energy and flair could only be sustained by a parallel lifestyle.

But then in the mid sixties, like so many European artists, Appel was abruptly shut off from 'sight' by the levelling impact of American art, which froze this image of Appel as Europe's 'capturer of the beast' in mid-action: a *déja vu*, which is now floating aimlessly but pervasively, disregarding the fact that both Appel and the world, in their different ways, have changed.

Appel was born in Amsterdam in 1921. Appel, and those who write about him attach much significance to the fact that he is by origin an Amsterdammer, an artist of the city.

> The vernacular of the city, including its children's graffiti, would inspire his imagery and his ideal would be one of absolute freedom from the strictures of overworked European minds. Dore Ashton, 1983

Amsterdam establishes Appel's primitivism (within the multitude of primitivisms prevalent in Europe after the war) as urban in character, a primitivism tainted with the realism of the city, proposing as the analogue for his art the pavement compositions of the street-wise urchin rather than those of the pre-industrial, noble and Nordic savage that prevailed, especially among the Danes in the Cobra group. And Appel clearly remembers the difficulty he had relating to their work: "It was too much like Nordic fables for me. It had nothing to do with being busy with the world, with life, with the people, with our time, as Van Gogh did, as Rembrandt did. The Danes had no background, no tradition. They had only myths and Danish fables. Jorn was the only one who eventually rose above that, probably because he lived for most of his life in Germany and Paris."

Amsterdam also explains why the art of Appel, a Northerner, appears so sensual, robust and unpuritanical; without any trace of conflict between the idealism of the mind and the demands of the world and the body: "I am a Dutchman, that is true. But Amsterdam is an island cut off from the rest of Holland. Holland is a puritanical Protestant country and Amsterdam is an atheistic, anarchistic, cosmopolitan city. Amsterdam is a strange mixture of blood and temperaments. I am of mixed blood. My mother's side of the family was French Huguenot and my father's side was German Dutch. Then there is the Spanish presence still lingering from the Spanish occupation of the Netherlands. You must not forget that since the Middle Ages, Amsterdam has been the cauldron of Europe."

The son of a barber in one of Amsterdam's working class districts, Appel attended the Dutch Academy of Fine Arts from 1940 to 1943 where he painted like "everyone else, with fine brushes and varnish making fine likenesses." But after the war he was to make a rapid acquaintance with modern art. It started with an exhibition of Picasso's wartime paintings, seen at the Stedelijk in 1945, with the grossly distorted face of Dora Maar setting the tone for the show. The intensity of Picasso's form was tempered when Appel came under the influence of Matisse, towards the end of 1947: "The form of Picasso and the red of Matisse," Appel says of his work of this time.

But Picasso and Matisse gave way to Dubuffet and Kurt Schwitters. Appel sees Schwitters as his most enduring influence, an influence which gave rise to the work of his first maturity, the series of wooden reliefs, *Questioning the Children*. The influence of Schwitters also led him to the *objets trouvés*, free standing assemblages of similar bits and pieces found in the streets which he would likewise paint in bright primary colors. Schwitters' art was an art of the streets, a deep lesson for Appel. Later on when he went to the United States he saw artists like Rauschenberg doing the same thing. "They made it bigger and more colorful, but as far as I could see the spirit was all Schwitters."

In 1948, the Dutch Experimental Group was formed, motivated largely by Constant Nieuwenhuys, an artist and later architect, who, two years before, had been to Denmark and met Asger Jorn and other Danish artists and was fired by their enthusiasm for groups, manifestos, and modern art. The group consisted of Appel, his friend Corneille, Anton Rooskens, Theo Wolvecamp and Constant's brother, Jan Nieuwenhuys. And then a year later, according to one of the more concise accounts of the birth of the COBRA movement, "they came into contact with other groups in Belgium and France which had developed out of Surrealism, but were opposed to the older established Surrealists, and wanted to arrive at an International Revolutionary Surrealism. During a meeting for this purpose in Paris, the Danish, the Dutch and the Belgian participants broke away to establish the COBRA group."

Appel is pleased at the upsurge and intensity of the current interest in COBRA, especially with the big show in Paris recently. "In the early fifties they weren't interested," he says. Those were years dominated by the abstract painters of the post-war *école de Paris* composed intially by those who, in the wake of the desolation of the war and the occupation, had opted for "order," for an equilibirum of form and spirit as proposed by Mondrian and De Stijl in the 1930s, and a little later on, by those who had transformed and diluted Fautrier's raw, aggressive manipulations of line and texture into the more tasteful "lyricism of decay."

COBRA was perhaps more of an idea than a group. "We only came together when we had shows. Otherwise we hardly saw one another. We were too busy trying to eke out a living, to find money to eat and to paint. When we did come together we had language problems. The Danes spoke Danish. The Belgians spoke French. And we spoke Dutch. I learned French later on. But it was too late. COBRA had ceased to exist. We missed the chance to chat to each other." But the idea of COBRA was intense. "The world was against us. We lived in countries where they didn't like our work. We were busy with COBRA as if it were a magnified image of ourselves. Every day brought discoveries. It was a red hot period. We even had the impression that we might be absolutely unique."

Studio in Paris, rue Brézin, 1956.

In fact Appel only ever met Asger Jorn three of four times in his life. The other Danes he met only once. "The Danes were very close knit as a group. I suppose it was inevitable. Denmark is a very small country." His relationship with the Belgians was better, especially with Christiaan Dotremont, the spokesman for COBRA, whom he saw from time to time at his house in Brussels. Appel admired Jorn's enormous energy: "He was obsessed with the idea of creating an international group of artists that would show together. I didn't much like the idea. He was always making groups. Later on in Germany he also tried to make little groups."

Recently much has been written about the relationship of COBRA to the new European and particularly German expressionism. Predictably, Appel himself sees very little connection. For him the element of despair, the overwhelming sense of desolation in the new German painting stands like a gulf between the two movements. In this regard Appel is very much struck with Anselm Keifer's work. "There is a great sentiment, great feeling in his painting. A sense of something smoldering, of something that is burnt out but is still smelling. A burnt out world where nothing grows." With COBRA there is a vitality, an underlying optimism. "During the war everything was closed up. Later, the borders opened and all we wanted to do was come alive, to discover a new space, a new landscape, a new image. That is what motivated us. With these Germans there is a powerful sense of being at the end of something." Appel admits that he is always aware of the sense of fear in contemporary Europe. "I don't feel it at all in the United States. It is a fear of war. I was recently in Germany and made my first visit to Berlin, where I was shown the Berlin Wall. The tension was unbearable. Barbed wire, soldiers, police, guard dogs. It was like a concentration camp. And it is this that informs the paintings of the new German artists."

In 1950 Appel left Amsterdam for Paris. "Corneille, Constant and I got thoroghly fed up with this Holland, which treated us like outcasts. The cunning tricks and narrowmindedness of the newspapers upset us to a greater extent than we wanted to admit. The three of us decided to go to Paris. If we had to live as vagabonds we could do it just as well there as in Holland." In 1951, after a final exhibition at the Palais des Beaux Arts in Liege, the COBRA group disbanded.

In retrospect, Appel's experience of the

Drawing, 1952

COBRA group appears as a period of acquaintance with the ins and outs of an aesthetic which
was more evident in the statements he made
about the paintings of this period (1949-51)
than in the paintings themselves. It was only in
the years after COBRA that Appel was to
develop and realise the COBRA precepts of
"spontaneity" and "directness." The work before that, for example *Maternity* 1951, is characterised by a childlike schematic drawing:
stick figures which divide the canvas into areas
of flat, timidly-textured primary color, with a
very clear separation of figure and ground.
Today it is difficult to reconcile these pleasant,
rather touching paintings with the aggressive
slogans of COBRA which were really a fore-
taste of work, in the cases of Appel and Jorn,
that was to follow three or four years later.
Comparing a work like *Maternity* 1951, with
Animal of the Earth 1955, the development in
Appel's work is immediately obvious. It is a
shift towards a format of kinaesthesia (which
COBRA never ceased to proclaim): the
manipulation of the paint reconstitutes for the
viewer Appel's muscular and emotional
rhythms during the act of creation. The canvas
becomes a repository for an unqualified, unrestrained sensation of movement and color. Ap-

pel achieves here what Constant, prompted by an exhibition of children's art at the Stedelijk in 1946, prophesied:

> ...enormous creative forces slumber in man's nature. We shall open a way for the activation of these forces by a destruction of the last formalisms which stand in the way of development.

Appel refers to these paintings as his "faces-places," "...Semi abstract compositions in which I tried to express forcefully the great conflict, the great problem of our time: the confrontation between technological man and nature...it was the world events, violence, famines, the memory of the death camps which were reflected in my paintings, often against my will." In these paintings confused mannerisms. He was in a rut. "I wanted to burn my old image, all that had been known hitherto as 'Appel's paintings.'" Then at a friend's house in New York he came across a book about Van Gogh, with photographs featuring magnified details of the paintings. He was struck by the rigorous organisation of the brushstrokes, the combination of freedom and discipline. This impression went deep. "Van Gogh was too familiar to me when I was young. It was easy to ignore him, to forget all about him. Then I saw these enlargements. What struck me about Van

Gogh then, in addition to his temperament and character, was the example he gives us of will-power and asceticism, while losing none of his liberty and spontaneity." Appel resolved to base the construction and the organisation of his paintings around the flat brush with its rectangular strokes. He turned to landscape. "I'd looked at so many trees, not only in nature, but in art. What a variety! And how many different ways of painting them! My dream was to show the tree's secret dimension, show that in it which is almost invisible but which is precisely what makes for its powerful presence. For me the tree is a facet of eternity, a manifestation of the eternal recurrence." Each of these paintings is a mosaic of choppy, rectangular strokes, arranged rhythmically across the canvas. Extending out of this, he started painting still-lifes, images which grew out of the vibrating patterns of flat brush-strokes. "The flat brush starts with nothing and finishes with nothing, but as a result of its movements you have an atmosphere, a dimension, full of rhythm and forms. I started doing still-lifes, because at that time everything seemed to me a still-life. I painted flowers, cats, heads, and more or less abstract things that the brushstrokes discovered for me."

Into the eighties, Appel began his series of window paintings, usually with simply the frame and pane as image. In these rectangular, latticed compositions he toned down his colour, producing the most abstract and contemplative paintings of his career. "I often walk in the lower downtown area of New York, the poor Jewish section. Here the windows are painted with left-over paint to protect them against the rain. The people use any color that they can get. So the windows are done in a crazy polychrome, unselfconsciously, with often vibrant and beautiful effects. I went to the South of France to think about it, to think about windows. You look through a window to the sea, to the landscape. The window makes a frame around the landscape. So when you isolate it it is already an object. The subject becomes an object through the window. I started to paint a space within a space. you look through the window at a space. And around the window is another space. So I paint three spaces. The space of the landscape or whatever, the space of the window, and the third space around the window. The color, the brush strokes, the drawing must bring out the interaction of these three spaces. Every artist who has lived near the Mediterranean has painted windows.

Picasso, Bonnard, Matisse, Léger, all painted windows."

His experience of New York, a city to which he has a deep attachment, became another of his subjects. "In New York I feel most at home. The whole way of life suits me. It was home the first day I stepped off the boat after eight days at sea. The people from the Martha Jackson Gallery were waiting for me. From the quay we drove right into the streets." Recently he has painted the squalor and the misery of the Bowery. In these works he has reintroduced a Picassoesque figuration and, for the first time in his art, aspects of narrative; often paintings with two or more figures interacting: tramps warming themselves over fires in the streets, old ladies walking their dogs in the slums. Nowadays, Appel is determined to engage the human condition in more explicit terms. Among his painterly meditations on New York is a series entitled *Crime* in which he attempts to come to terms with the violence of the city. There are also paintings with titles like *Sick Bed, At The Tomb* and of concentration camp scenes, figures cowering behind barbed wire. "I have paintings in my studio which nobody has seen. Recently, I finished a tryptych called *Hunger and War*, about starvation in the third

Drawing, 1980

world." Accompanying these are imaginary portraits of Mahler, Kafka, Gertude Stein and Sartre. "Let's say that the new creative eruption we are witnessing everywhere should be tempered with severe meditation because what our time needs more than anything is a more rigorous language."

The recent years have been a period of crisis and transition for Appel. Although there have been major changes in his work, its central aspect, that of improvisation, remains. For all his attempts to reconstitute it, his art is still firmly rooted within a format of a childlike spontaneity and innocence; qualities which are rarely able to accommodate the tragic without coming dangerously close to melodrama. One is often too quickly seduced by the colour, the lush textures, the childlike buoyancy of the drawing to appreciate the sense of tragedy that Appel is trying to convey in paintings like the *Sick Bed* 1981. Paradoxically, the very best of the work derives its authority from his valiant attempts to go into the face of this unsuitability as in *The Tomb* 1981, when he strains and contorts an aesthetic based on innocence and affirmation to convey a note of despair. This has not gone unnoticed by Appel's commentators. JJ Sweeney has referred to Appel's depiction of violence in New York as "happy crimes."

For me, Appel's most successful works have been the recent paintings, especially the landscapes and the window paintings; precisely because their reductive and structured formats can accommodate him as an "adult" and allow him to express adult emotions. Tragedy, despair, are emotive states too layered and reflective to be adequately conveyed through an aesthetic founded on the visceral sensibility and the spontaneous, unreflective enthusiasms of a child. But Appel's need and determination to arrive at an art more responsive to the times endow these paintings with a compelling character which is overwhelming and which transforms all contradictions and inadequacies into 'living' contradictions and inadequacies: each a testimony to a powerful and exemplary urge to be relevant.

Untitled , 1984, acrylic, oil stick, paper collage

Sir Alan Bowness

APPEL
by Alan Bowness

1986

Drawing, 1955

It is a commonplace that art has changed radically in the 1980s, and the new sensibility and awareness of painterly and expressive qualities now felt by everyone forces us to revalue the recent past. It thus becomes clearer than ever that one of the giants of the 1950s was the Dutch painter, Karel Appel, and in this changed climate it is a particular pleasure to note that Appel himself, now in his sixties, has responded with some of the most interesting work being done anywhere today.

I first saw these new pictures in Appel's New York studio a few years ago. For once the life in the streets outside had come straight through into the paintings, and here was someone grappling directly with the undercurrent of violence and aggression that is a constant feature of living in New York—or for that matter elsewhere. Appel was painting the drunks and junkies and beggars that haunt the sidewalks, but translating these realistic images into myth, in a monumental, almost apocalyptic way. So the beggars become universal figures, and the largest painting in the exhibition, *War and Hunger*, is, according to the artist, about starvation in the Third World.

Appel is concerned with big moral and personal issues, but it's done in a very straightforward fashion, without preaching, and entirely through the language of the paint. "I have no principles", Appel says, "I opt for life"; and even if the figure is absent, as it is in the "Cloud" paintings, the presence of the living and the natural is always strongly felt.

Indeed it's this passionate humanism and the sensual feeling for paint and colour that have always characterised Appel's work. We remember that he is the countryman of Van Gogh, and that like Van Gogh, Appel had to leave his native Holland to fulfil himself. The effect that his early paintings made in the 1950s will never be forgotten by those who saw them—and I am delighted that the Tate Gallery now owns one of the masterpieces of this period, *People, Birds and Sun* of 1954. At the time Herbert Read wrote of Appel that "No painter of his generation has made a greater impact on the artistic consciousness of Europe...the reason is not far to seek. It lies in the power and directness of the images he has created".

It is clear from this exhibition that Appel is again creating powerful images. We are privileged to see the new work, which shows that he is once more at the top of his form.

Drawing, 1955

Horse Series; The Rider, 1983, 30½ × 43″, collage, acrylic, paper

KAREL APPEL:
"I'M JUST MESSING AROUND"
by Mariette Josephus Jitta

1982

The Cattle Slaughter, 1981, 59 × 39½", acrylic, oilstick, ink, paper

"A painter with a keen sense of color fixes his gaze on the canvas, his mouth is half open, he pants, his palette is a chaos of paint. He dips his brush in this chaos, his work is wrested from the chaos. . . He stands up, puts himself at a distance, looks, sits down again . . . tests, alters, changes, ravages his colors." This quotation evokes an image of an artist obsessed with mastering his materials— the brushes, the paints on the palette— his creative deed represented as an obsessive preoccupation to the exclusion of all else, as the heaving chest and sagging jaw emphasize.

It could have been a description of the artist at work in the film *The Reality of Karel Appel*, but in fact it occurs in *Essais sur la peinture*, written by the French philosopher Diderot in 1766.[1]

The Reality of Karel Appel was made in 1961 by Jan Vrijman. The film shows an intensified image of the artist as conceived by Diderot: the painter in action, surrounded by pots and tubes of paint, brushes and palette knives, pieces of cloth and cardboard. "The outside world seemed to be shut out and gone, leaving only the studio space in which Appel attacked the white canvas, almost nine meters square, as if he had to master a gigantic wild beast."[2] The film recorded the way in which the painting originated; it illustrated a manner of working which had earlier been summed up by Appel as *"I'm just messing around."*

What is the meaning of such a statement, made on a momentary impulse? Is it a wry joke, or is it indicative of a way of dealing with art, implying a certain attitude towards possibilities and conceptions of making art? It is both. I shall make some comments on this below that have to do with the label that was attached to Appel as if he were some sort of clown "just messing around."

One thing is clear: Appel did make that famous statement, and in doing so he created an image of himself—an image of the artist who knows neither rules nor conventions, who sets to work without any restraint whatsoever, naively and intuitively—or, that is how he wishes to be seen by others.

His statement was obviously aimed at a public. For it was a confirmation of what many people had known "all along"—his art was indeed a "mess". "Blots, splashes, smears" was the resounding headline of a Dutch newspaper when the first large-scale exhibition of Cobra artists (Appel was one of them) opened in the Amsterdam Stedelijk Museum in 1949.[3]

The phrase "messing around" clearly matched the image of a specific type of artist, in this case Karel Appel. Speculations about artists—their character, their behavior—are by no means a new phenomenon. They have led to the most divergent conceptions of the artist, ranging from that of tempestuous paint-thrower (Appel) to that of the cool disciplined scientist (Mondrian).[4] Such notions have been described as a composite of "myth and reality, of conjectures and observations, of make-believe and experience."[5] They owe their existence to artists and public alike, and the latter, significantly, includes writers.

Contingent on Diderot's conception of the artist are the images which arose in the nineteenth century—notably in the Romantic period—and which still exist today. The most famous of these occurs in Balzac's *Le Chef-d'oeuvre Inconnu (The Unknown Masterpiece)*, first published in 1831. I mention it here because it is with that specific image that modern artists in particular have identified themselves or have been identified by others[6]. Balzac, too, describes a tempestuous artist, who "worked with such passionate ardor that the perspiration stood on his bald head; all his motions were so impatient and abrupt that it seemed. . . that there must be a devil in his body, acting through his hands and forcing them to perform all sorts of fantastic actions against the man's will."[7] Moreover his eyes flashed in a supernatural manner, and his gestures and exclamations were spasmodic and convulsive: Paf! paf! paf! pon! pon! pon![8]

But besides his flamboyant and erratic behavior, the true artist possessed other characteristics. "He displays the good qualities with which Nature has endowed him without ostentation, the bad qualities without shame" (Diderot).[9] He is immoral, malevolent, unsociable, greedy, filthy, and extravagant all at once. Both Diderot and Balzac associated all these characteristics with genius.

Another aspect of this image of the creative genius is the idea that the artist is free to act but not to think. A painter should paint, not speak, Goethe maintained. In *The Unknown Masterpiece* the young Poussin is warned against becoming entangled in theories: "prac-

tice and observation are everything to a painter, so that, if rhetoric and poetry quarrel with
the brush, we reach the doubting stage...."[10]
(But Balzac was also convinced that no masterpiece could ever originate *without* doubt).

Artists who take up the pen as well as the
paintbrush tend to arouse suspicion, at least as
far as their penmanship is concerned. Kandinsky, who was both artist and theorist, once
complained: "People want the artist to paint
continually and exclusively, certainly not to
write, not even letters. They would even have
him eat with a brush instead of a fork, if that
were possible."[11] In that respect, too, Appel
reassures his public: he does not theorize, he
"just messes around," even though he eats with
knife and fork.

But the image of the painter wresting his
work "from the chaos of his palette" in a state of
diabolical fervor differs from the corresponding image of the poet or writer—although
there, too, we find plenty of testimonies of
poems being composed in a state of somnam-
bulism.

Diderot believed that the painter gave much
more of himself in his work than the writer.[12]
But even if this is so, it does not account for the
discrepancy. A possible explanation is the

Studio in Paris, rue Brézin, 1956.

following: a painting or sculpture always bears the traces of the physical action that went into its making, even when the artist has made every effort to conceal or erase them; painting and sculpture are associated, as a matter of course, with physical action and exertion. And herein lies the difference with the writer: his work appears in print; it seldom if ever recalls a manuscript spattered with ink and crossed-out works, or even a closely-typed sheet of paper. The idea of the quill dipped in ink is romantic, certainly, but it is usually soon forgotten. But the smears and blots, coagulated drippings of paint directly squeezed from the tube onto the canvas, the furrows of palette knives and brushes, the imprint of fingers or of the palm of the hand in Appel's paintings, do not let the viewer forget for one moment that they were made by hand, that there is a highly personal, immediate relationship between the action of making and the result; no printer, no machine, has come into play. As soon as this is the case the work loses its potency, all the beautiful books with high-quality reproductions of Appel's paintings notwithstanding, and could not a large section of his public see "right away," simply by looking at the reproduction, that it was all just a mess?

In the foregoing, I have said much more about the making of art—or rather about a certain idea thereof—than about the art itself. Appel's "messing around" is, after all, a statement about the making and not about the result.

In *The Unknown Masterpiece*, the old artist, whose feverish animation I referred to earlier, shows his two friends, both of whom are artists, the canvas that he has been working on for the last ten years. Instead of the portrait of a woman that both of them expect, *La Belle Noiseuse*, they see nothing but "colors piled upon one another in confusion, and entangled in a multitude of curious lines."[13] The old man points out eyes and nose, light and shade, and takes the outrage of his two friends for a sign of confusion at the sight of such perfection. But disillusion was inevitable: the old man destroys his picture and kills himself.

Karel Appel was born in 1921 in Amsterdam, almost a century after publication of Balzac's *The Unknown Masterpiece* (1831) and about ten years after Kandinsky painted his *First Abstract Watercolor*, the work that is—albeit for the sake of convenience—generally taken to mark the beginning of abstract art (1910). In other words, Appel started working at a time when abstract art was already a fact. Even though a large section of the public, as was certainly the case in the fifties, sees his work as nothing but "colors piled upon one another in confusion, and entangled in a multitude of curious lines", or in other words, "a mess", he has been spared the sad fate of his predecessor in *The Unknown Masterpiece*.

Nonetheless, in 1957 a Dutch newspaper announced that "Mr. Appel belongs to the artistic underworld; his work lacks a true tension and superhuman commitment,"[14] a statement which is by no means mild, especially when one considers that the mythological underworld is the realm of the dead.

The "superhuman commitment"—again!— belongs to a specific conception of the artist and the making of art. Now we can also raise the question, of course, of how these "colors piled upon one another" come about, and subsequently whether this manner of so-called "messing around" or handling of the plastic means, color and line, also fits in with a certain tradition. Artists have in the past made statements concerning this subject, although not in great detail. Usually they don't say how "it" is made and what they do say is inextricably linked with the image that they want to project.

Here, too, a blending of "myth and reality" is inevitable.

"For me a tube of paint is a rocket" was the headline of two Dutch newspapers in January and September 1957. This statement of Appel's is just as elucidating as the art-critical commentary pronounced by a contemporary of the Impressionists: "They shoot the paint on the canvas with pistols."[15]

Finally, let me illustrate my point with a story about the German Expressionist painter Emil Nolde. It occurs in the *Memoirs* of another German artist, Georg Grosz, and took place around 1910, before the amazed eyes of the art students at the Dresden academy: "Nolde did not paint any more with brushes. Under the spell of inspiration, he said, he had thrown away his brushes, he had soaked his old paint-rag in paint and had swept it over the canvas in a state of blissful exaltation. In the light of tradition, his paintings were shapeless and primitive; craft had been neglected, inner expression was all; next to a Rembrandt or Raphael it was a wild orgy of smears...We young people were enthusiatic. At last we could smear to our hearts' content—ha!—take to task all the rules about complementary colors. Was not life itself a rag soaked in full complementary colors?."[16] Nolde's rags and Appel's rockets/tubes can hardly be described as being relevant for their manner of working. But they are on the one hand an expression of a desire and expectation concerning painting itself, on the other hand they attest to great enthusiasm. Indeed, the latter was, according to Diderot, the primary requirement of creative action; Balzac even spoke of "un noble enthousiasme."[17]

In October, 1950, Appel wrote a letter to the architect Aldo van Eyck. He was in Paris at the time, having arrived two months earlier in the company of two other young artists, Constant and Corneille. In this letter he refers to his work—there is no reporter present to "note it all down"—saying: ". . . now I paint blotches larger larger blotches of color endlessly over each other, removing, new streaks of color, until there is a concentrated plane. . . ."[18] These words provide some insight into Appel's working method. They are furthermore reflected in the paintings and drawings he made in those years: now a teeming conglomerate of small streaks of color, smudges and dabs (*Dog*), then again broad, vigourous brush-strokes and blots of paint in a network of delicate lines and rapid scratches (*Festive City*).

The gouache *Festive City* recalls some of the drawings and watercolors that Appel made before he left Amsterdam: the children's balloon *Parade*, the *Questioning Children*, and *Children Playing in the Water*). Yet this gouache is not representational. It was given a title as an afterthought, or, to quote Paul Klee, it was "baptised." Klee regarded this "baptism" as the final act in making a work of art. Such a title has, for Klee just as for Appel, nothing to do with a predetermined motif: it is evoked purely by the forms and colors, which originated by his own hand. And when, in the case of Appel, the same work is referred to as *Wall Drawing* in one book and as *Personnage dans le Brouillard* in the next, this simply means that, like every combination of forms and colors, it can evoke a variety of associations. This applies both to the maker and to the viewer. Where one person recognizes a figure in the mist, the next perceives an upturned wastepaper basket or a "mess". But this need not affect their appreciation of the work.

Festive City can, partly because of the title, evoke associations with decorated streets, a square festooned with lanterns, but the work can just as well suggest simply light and gaiety, because Appel did not set out to depict anything in particular. But this is seldom the case. The colors and lines emerging on the canvas or paper in the process of making evoke images in Appel's mind, images that take possession, as it were, of the blots and stains of color, giving them direction—". . . endlessly over each other and new streaks of color." This direction can in turn change by "removing, and new streaks of color," in which other images arise. "I always," Appel wrote, "spontaneously started out abstractly, with dashes and brushstrokes which I destroyed again later. I was *full*, I looked at it, the matter triggered my imagination, resembled everything. . . ."[19]

In this way of handling the "matter"—paint and canvas—and the concentrated observation of what it produces, the possibility exists up to the very last moment of the imagination taking command. This is how Appel's world of wondrous creatures emerges: animals and birds with human traits, people as beasts, vulnerable, aggressive, exuberant and laughable.

The "matter. . . resembled everything," according to Appel. He is referring to the ability to perceive objects and images in random forms, which are, strictly speaking, totally unrelated to them. Psychologists speculate about this ability with their ink-blots (Rorschach tests); painters and writers exploit it. And who did not, as a child, see bears in the clouds and birds in the wallpaper? In *Kind tussen Vier Vrouwen* (Child Between Four Women), Simon Vestdijk describes how the boy, before falling asleep, sees "the wallpaper, bluish green, with flower-like figures, which he counted, and fixed with his gaze, enveloping, enlacing, taking apart again, or transfiguring into faces—these faces never grew to be complete, each newly-made eye meant the loss of a mouth, or else started squinting when he added the ears. . . ."[20]

In his treatise on painting, Leonardo da Vinci (1452-1519) advised artists to observe walls stained with damp and stones of uneven color, for they can give the imagination countless suggestions. Looking at them the artist can see "likeness of divine landscapes, adorned with mountains, ruins, rock, woods, great plains, hills and valleys in great variety. . . battlefields and strange figures, in violent action, expressions of faces and clothes. . . " (Incidentally, Vasari mentions that a contemporary of Da Vinci's preferred to look at "*un muro dove lungamente fusse stato sputato da persone malate*").[21] Leonardo's advice was duly followed by painters, or they referred to him in defence of their own working method. A second, supplementary condition, to which Leonardo attached equal importance, however, was overlooked by some. While blots of paint applied at random to the canvas may well give inspiration, they cannot give guidance as to how the painting should be completed. However fascinating they may stimulate the painter's imagination, they are no more than a means, subject to scrupulous deliberation and execution. And the painter who does not fully take this into account, "makes the most wretched landscapes," according to Leonardo.[22]

The English artist Alexander Cozens (1717-1786) was a painter of landscapes. He devised a new method of making them, convinced that Leonardo would have approved. In 1785 he published *A New Method of Assisting the Invention in Drawing Original Compositions of Landscapes*. The new technique could be summed up in one word: "blotting". Cozens wrote: "to blot is to make varied spots producing accidental forms from which ideas are presented to the mind...to sketch is to delineate ideas; blotting suggests them."[23] His idea aroused a lot of laughter, because "blotting" was just as ridiculous as "messing around". Cozens' method amounted to covering the canvas at random with blots and streaks, in which he then discerned a landscape which he finally elaborated, mostly in a strictly conventional manner.

Cozens would no doubt have been surprised to encounter a like-minded artist in the seventeenth-century Dutch painter Jan van Goyen, if at least there is any truth in the story that Samuel van Hoogstraaten recounted in his *Inleyding tot de Hooge Schoole der Schilderconst*, published in 1678 in Rotterdam. Hoogstraten tells of a competition held by three painters. Each of them was to make a painting in one day. The demand for paintings was great at the time, "which incited some painters to practise painting rapidly, indeed to produce one picture each day." One of these painters, Knipbergen, worked extremely quickly: "sky, horizon, trees, mountains and foaming waterfalls fell from his brush as the letters from the pen of a copyist. . ." Jan van Goyen set to work quite differently: "Having roughly swabbed his entire panel with paint, here light, there dark, till it looked like a streaked agate stone, or marbled paper, he then perceived all sorts of curious things in the paint. . . which he made apparent with small touches. . . ," his eyes being trained to recognise "figures. . . which lay hidden in a chaos of paint."[24] When reflecting on Van Goyen's "overswabbing of the panel" as the first stage in making his landscape, one cannot help thinking of the abstract blots and stains with which Appel states his canvases. Did not the first touches have, for both painters, concealed in their midst" all sorts of curious things and figures?" A major difference between Jan van Goyen's *View of Dordrecht* and Karel Appel's *Festive City* is, however, that in Appel's case the blots and streaks of color remain visible as such in the completed painting. In Van Goyen's case they disappeared in the carefully detailed depiction of the city along the river Jan van Goyen did not win the competition, but he did become famous. Knipbergen, whose ambition was to paint at great speed, was forgotten; the winner was Parselles, who "handled his brushes so slowly;" he made his landscape "in his mind first."

The aim to express themselves the way children, primitive peoples or the insane do, was a deliberate choice on the part of the artists. They were neither children, nor primitive, nor insane; they merely saw in the visual expres-

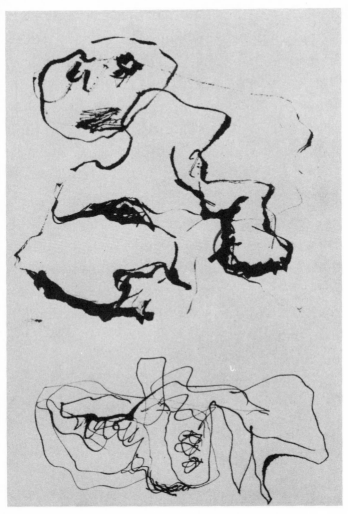

Drawing, 1952, ink on paper

sions of such people that certain possibilities had been realised which were related to their own intentions. It was with these possibilities that they concerned themselves: the little boy grew up to become a lawyer or civil servant, while they became artists by profession. In other words, the little boy would at most doodle a web of lines or stick-men during his interminable meetings, or, at best, he might become a Sunday-painter. And there, too, he would find the artist at his side: Kandinsky admired the works of Le Douannier Rousseau (1844-1910), the French self-taught artist who painted without training, without knowledge of academic rules and regulations. Kandinsky compared the artist to a child, who naturally and naively, without artifice, finds the right forms and colors. Indeed, in giving a few of his abstract compositions the title "Improvisation," he was stressing this point, too.

It is not my intention here to dwell on the ways in which artists during this century have concerned themselves with the expressions of children, primitive peoples, and the mentally ill. It is enough to mention that interest in such expressions has increased largely due to abstract art. Form and color in this kind of art are no longer tied down to phenomena derived from visible reality; they are "just" forms and colors which have been brought together and arranged in a certain way. They are judged exclusively on these grounds, good or bad. The same criteria could now be applied to images created in remote primitive cultures; they, too, could be appreciated as an exciting assemblage of colors and shapes divorced from all representational values or meanings.

The appreciation for this quality, however, went hand in hand with a fascination for the representation itself. Even if the true significance escaped the artists, they saw in these images the visualisation of universal characteristics. The interest in children's drawings—so explicit among the Cobra painters—was confirmed in an exhibition devoted to such drawings which was held in the same year as the first big Cobra show, in 1949, and in the same museum, the Amsterdam Stedelijk Museum. As Constant wrote in *Reflex*, "the exhibition of children's drawings has shown once again what an enormous creative potential slumbers in the nature of man."[37] He was convinced that the potential of the child's unrestricted creative expression remains present as a natural ability, although admittedly

Drawing, 1980

suppressed, in the grown man. In his book *Bildnerei der Geisteskranken*, Prinzhorn explained the origin of every visual expression as the joint product of different motives, any one of which can dominate in a work of art, or conversely, be absent.[38] As one of these motives he mentioned the desire to play, playing being conceived as any activity without a specific practical goal. The two main characteristics of play in the visualising action—the creation of an image—are, according to Prinzhorn, on the one hand the urge to draw, which finds expression in its simplest form in thoughtless doodling and scribbling, and on the other hand the ability to recognize images in these scribblings or, in other words, to see "all sorts of curious things and figures." The works of the Cobra painters are permeated with this sense of play; they felt an affinity with the child at play, in this case: drawing. "In each man a child is hidden: that child wants to play."[39] The Cobra artists sought, in their work, to stimulate the child within them.

After the disbanding of Cobra in 1951, Appel continued to deal with the same subjects, even though his images were now evoked in a vehement, dynamic handwriting *Personage*, and *Human Landscape*.

The streaks and smears of paint become more and more prominent, they dominate the sheet, they are like the leftovers of paint on the palette which remain, bearing witness to the creative deed. In connection with Kandinsky and Appel, I have already mentioned the important role which they ascribed to the material in what Dotremont called "the drama and play of painting."[40] This is accompanied—in Kandinsky's case less manifestly than in that of Appel—by the increasing concern for the way the game is played, i.e. for the action of painting. Degas called painting *"une série d'opérations,"*[41] in Appel's works these *opérations* remain clearly visible. In this respect his work fits in with the most striking development in the art of the fifties. This movement was given various names, such as Abstract Expressionism, Action Painting, or *Tachisme* (*tâche* being the French word for "stain"). The movement had as many variations as it had members, who were, rightly or wrongly, referred to as abstract expressionists, action painters or *tachistes*. But they all had one thing in common. For these artists, the process of making art is just as important as the result—and sometimes it is even all-important. This process begins by "placing a white canvas on the easel" (Constant),[42] or laying a huge piece of linen on the floor (as did the American painter Jackson Pollock). On this ground the first blots and streaks, scribbles and "overswabbings" are applied, randomly and intuitively. They are the product of movements of the arm, or the result of paint dripping on and over the canvas. As in a chain reaction, the painting takes shape. One color evokes the next, each streak leading to another blot, until the painting is finished. This more or less automatic manner of painting was employed by some artists constantly throughout their working process, while others left open the possibility of deliberate, preconceived intervention in the process. All of them, however, like Nolde (an action painter "*avant la lettre*," as it were) may finally find themselves standing before the result in amazement—and others with them.[43] Those "others" can see the impulses and gestures of the artist in the painted result, at least if they are so inclined, for they can also dismiss it as "just messing around." The concern for the process of making is the outcome of a development intiated in part by Kandinsky. This development cannot be described here. It is perhaps fitting to conclude with a quotation of Paul Valéry, the French writer for whom the execution of a work was, equally, a work of art.[44] He stated in a lecture held in 1933, "Passive enjoyment tires and bores us we also need the pleasure of doing (*'le laisir de faire'*). Strange pleasure, complex pleasure, pleasure interspersed with torments, with effort: nor is our seeking after this pleasure devoid of obstacles and bitterness, doubts and despair."[45] Rather than seeing the works of Karel Appel as a mess, it would be better to see them as the outcome of his pleasure in painting. Postscript: Appel did not go to the extremes described by Hoogstraaten: "Kornelis Ketel, in order to demonstrate that the master, not the brush, is the artist, did some very good pieces with his fingers instead of with brushes; and not being satisfied with the result, proceeded to paint some things with his right foot and others with his left."[46]

NOTES

1. Diderot, *Oeuvres Esthétiques*, P. Vernière, Paris, 1959, p. 574.
2. Jan Vrijman, *The Reality of Karel Appel*, 1971.
3. *Het Vrije Volk*, 1949, Willemijn L. Stokvis, Cobra proefschrift, Utrecht 1973.
4. Exhibition catalog *Mondrian Drawings*, Stuttgart, Den Haag, Baltimore 1981, p. 263, 282.

5. Rudolf and Margot Wittkower, *Born under Saturn*, London, p. 294.

6. Dore Ashton, *A Fable of Modern Art*, London 1980.

7. Vrijman (as 2), p. 64.

8. Honoré Balzac, *Sarrasine*, Leipzig, Inselverlag, 1910, p. 342.

9. Diderot, *Rameau's Cousin*, Frankfurt 1968, p. 405, Otto Stelzer, *Die Vorgeschichte der abstrakten Kunst*, München, 1964, p. 139.

10. Balzac (as 8), p. 349.

11. Stelzer (as 9), p. 184.

12. Diderot (as 1), p. 675.

13. Balzac (as 8), p. 360.

14. *De Telegraaf*, 9/24/1957.

15. Werner Hofmann, *Grundlagen der modernen Kunst*, Stuttgart, 1966, p. 230.

16. Hofmann (as 15), p. 266.

17. Balzac, *Le Chef-d'oeuvre inconnu*, Paris 1891, p. 2, Ashton (as 6), p. 11.

18. *Karel Appel Tegen Simon Vinkenoog*, in Haagse Post, 5/16/1957; Simon Vinkenoog, *Het verhaal van Karel Appel*, Utrecht 1963, p. 78.

19. Vinkenoog (as 18), p. 148.

20. S Vestdijk, *Kind tussen vier vrouwen*, Amsterdam 1975, p. 32.

21. E.H. Gombrich, *Art and Illusion*, London, 1962, p. 159, (quote Leonardo). Quote Vasari: Hubert Damisch, *Théorie du nuage*, Paris, 1972, p. 49.

22. Gombrich, 1967 (as 21), p. 217.

23. Ibid, p. 211.

24. Gombrich found this in *Samuel Hoogstraten, Inleyding tot de Hooge Schoole der Schilderconst*, Rotterdam, 1678, 237.

25. Emile Cardon in: *La Presse*, 4/29/1874; translation of *Jacques Lethève, Impressionistes et Symbolistes devant la presse*. Paris, 1959, p. 69.

26. Louis Leroy in: *Le Charivari*, 4/25/1874; translation of Lethève (as 25), p. 64f.

27. A.Th. (J.A. Alberdingk Thijm) in *De Amsterdammer*, 10/19/1884.

28. Kandinsky, *Gesammelte Schriften*, Vol. 1, edited by Hans K. Röthel and Jelena Hahl-Koch, Bern, 1980, p. 27f.

29. Hofmann (as 15), p. 138.

30. Kandinsky. *Rückblicke*, Bern, 1977, p. 22f. *Sonnenuntergang* compair Stelzer (as 9).

31. Translation of *Paul Valery, Degas danse dessin*, Paris (1938), 1965.

32. Emile Zola, *Le naturalisme au Salon*, in: Le Voltaire, June 1880, quoted: E. Zola, Mon salon, Manet, Ecrits sur l'art, Paris, 1970, p. 341.

33. Vinkenoog (as 19), p. 27, 31.

34. Stokvis (as 3), p. 68.

35. Hugo Claus, *Karel Appel schilder*, Amsterdam 1964; translation of quote: *Appel en Alechinsky, Zwart, met gedichten van Hugo Claus*,

Amsterdam 1978, poem XVIII.

36. Vinkenoog (as 18), p. 71.

37. Translation of J.L. Locher, *De schilderkunst van Constant*, catalog: *Constant. Schilderijen 1940-1980*, Haags Gemeentemuseum, Den Haag, 1980, p. 11.

38. H. Prinzhorn, *Bildnerei der Geisteskranken*, Berlin, 1968.

39. Nietzsche; motto of Christian Morgenstern, *Alle Galgenlieder*, Wiesbaden, 1979.

40. *Appel and Alechinsky* (as 35), p. 1.

41. Valéry (as 31), p. 9.

42. Translation of Locher (as 37), p. 21.

43. Hofmann (as 15), p. 259.

44. Stelzer (as 9), p. 220f.

45. Translation of Paul Valéry, *Petit discours aux peintres graveur*, in: Pièces sur l'art, Paris, 1962, p. 110.

46. Hoogstraten (as 24), p. 235.

A WAY TO SING ART
by Rudi H. Fuchs

1987

In the new paintings of Karel Appel there is still the old painterly sharpness and eloquence, the sure instinct for the right movement of line and the right burst of colour. But the new paintings are not just a newer or swifter version of the old ones. Karel Appel seems to have found a serene freedom which makes his recent work as calm and majestic as the sea or as the clouds in the sky.

They are paintings that need few words. They are an absolute joy to look at, and they show us that a great painter always finds a way to sing his art.

Donald Kuspit

GROWING YOUNGER
by Donald Kuspit

1987

I am convinced that it is hygienic—if I may use the word—to discover in death a goal towards which one can strive, and that shrinking away from it is something unhealthy and abnormal which robs the second half of life of its purpose.
C.G. Jung, *Freud and Psychoanalysis*, 1961

Fire, 1986, 96 × 76, oil on canvas

L ooking at these new works, one could say that Karel Appel has again become young. As with the early Cobra works which first brought him fame, we see a similar sombre vigor—brilliant color, but seen through a dark glass—and the same primitive, child-like handling, generating a complex texture as frightening as it is alluring. But the plot of ambivalence has taken a new turn, signified by the structural change in these works. It is most evident in their fragmentation: in the puppet-like sculptures (all 1987), the literal dismemberment of the figure; in the paintings (all 1986), the division of space into independent pictorial units, which do not add up to a narrative whole. It is also evident in a new emblematic tendency: for all the internal drama of the figures and scenes, there is a sense of crystallization of the image at odds with Cobra expressivity. There is still pathos, but it is pathos codifying itself.

In *Fire* the graffiti-crude figures in the upper

tier and the peasant in the lower tier are both stereotypical representations, almost to the point of being self-caricaturing cartoons. In *Bateau de Fous* a seemingly indiscriminate variety of images is used to praise folly and madness. In fact, while obviously not the same, conceptually the images all belong to the same family. They are different cards from the same ideational suite. The strategy is in fact medieval; but in Appel's pictures the "minor" narrative scenes have completely displaced the main event. There is none, only the pile up of images thrusting towards a single point. In the sculpture, the single giant figure seems to afford an overarching physical unity, but it too is deceptive. For limbs are missing or displaced, parts are outsized or undersized, the proportion between them is thrown off, even overtly absurd. Again, as with the paintings, the unity is conceptual. It has to do with what the grouping of parts symbolizes. Coming from different directions yet peculiarly similar in import, each part is an innuendo of the same basic unconscious meaning. The fact that each of Appel's works is an untotalizable constellation of elements already suggests that it is not a representation in the standard sense of the term—a translation of an already existing meaning. Instead, the radical incompleteness of the works suggests a meaning coming into being, an attitude taking form. The indeterminacy implied by the inherent incompleteness of the works suggests a struggle with an uncanny content, hard to express yet impossible to repress.

The content, I believe, is death. It is symbolically manifest through the fragmentation, and its effect of incompleteness and indeterminacy. The pull of death is responsible for the "brokenness" of these works. They formally carry forward the familiar 20th century esthetic of discontinuity/disjunctiveness/instability/disintegration, but with new purpose. It has been said that death is truly pornographic, which I take to mean that it is the really forbidden subject matter—the most resented, most tabooed reality. Sigmund Freud argued that we could not think our own death; it always turned out to be somebody else's death. Appel, I think, is trying, through symbols, to articulate his own death, and to find purpose in the thought of it. In these works he is moving towards unconscious acceptance of his death, if not exactly embracing it.

Appel's new works show the taking stock that comes with anticipation of death. It is as though Appel's life is flashing by him, both in ideological substance and vital texture. *The Indian Chief*, the feeling of being alone in *The Desert*, the fierce bull on *The Prairie*, *The Weightlifter* performing extraordinary artistic feats against the inertia of matter, the man who has returned to nature and become truly close to the animals of the *Country*, the madman on the *Bateau de Fous*, the maker of *Fire*(s)— Appel has been all these archetypal characters in his lifetime. Each is a personification of an aspect of himself. I would even venture to say that all of Appel's personalities would find their place on Jung's list of personifying archetypes.

At the approach of death, all the persons one has been pushily come forward, vividly manifest themselves. This is part of the involuntary taking stock which come with awareness of death. It involves recognition of one's limitations, that is, recognition of the limited number of roles one was able to play in life—one's limited being, which gives one's life only a certain number of meanings. The archetypes appear partly in inner acknowledgement of a certain fulfillment of the particular life roles they imply, but also to signal that one is about to abandon them—or be abandoned by them.

Ship of Fools, 1986, 96 × 76, oil on canvas

This is the meaning that is unconscious. The reason the self-personifications appear as conventions, or have a collective or impersonal look—which Appel's figures and scenes do, however constitued they are by his "personal" touch—is that, with the coming of death, they are revealed as not really belonging to one, not exclusively one's own. They belong to no one and to everyone; they are generic and general forms to be filled by the content of a particular person's life or to remain algebraically anonymous. They are universally present and possible unconsciously, if never completely actualized and something we are never completely conscious of. One fills the roles they represent with the content of one's own expressive person, every person expressing whatever roles are his or hers in different ways. With the approach of death, one comes to recognize this, and to intuit that one seems to exist for the archetypal role—have lived a "typical" life— rather than the role existing to express or fit one's individuality. It is this profound psychological recognition that Appel is articulating in these works.

Jung distinguishes between the sign and symbol. The one is a translation of a clear and distinct meaning, the other is an attempt to grasp an obscure meaning, out of reach in the unconscious. Symbols tend to be pictorial analogues, mediating unconscious meaning wordlessly. Of all unconscious meanings, that of death is more likely to be given in a spontaneous image than in conscious thought. It will have the innocent incoherence of a dream, and be dialectically balanced between personal content and collective form. Like Appel's dream pictures, it is more likely to be disjointed, if peculiarly dense, collection of parts than a seamless unity. Most of all, it will come in a disguise that seems its very substance.

I want to suggest that the famous "savagery" of Appel's handling has now become a disguise rather than an end in itself, as in the Cobra paintings. Appel has not lost his *Sturm und Drang* savagery, but it has become "classicized"—a savagery in the service of an ego that has the strength to recognize and accept its own death. It is this strength that Appel's fierceness now symbolizes—the strength to see fate without resigning oneself to it. This contrasts with the rage against and defiance of fate that Cobra savagery implied, however haunted it was by fate. That is, Appel's postwar Cobra painting was a fiery phoenix that creatively rose from the ashes of a destroyed

Europe but still had the dust of that destruction's pathos on its wings. It was an exemplary
instance of creation out of destruction. But
where Appel's early savagery was a sign of
conscious rebellion against death, the savagery of his current, late style is a symbol of an
unconsciously anticipated death.

This is perhaps most evident in the sculptures, where the masking—"tattooing"—of the
figure (if only the face in some of the nudes),
seems to entomb it. In Appel's Cobra paintings
the figure was inherently expressive; expressivity was revelatory of its essential
bodiliness. In Appel's sculptures expressivity
tends to obscure bodiliness. When the body's
nakedness is photographically present, as in
the nudes that are incompletely painted, the
naked and painted parts disjunct, in a further
symbolic fragmentation.

The sculptural nudes are special works.
They fall into two groups, those with heads
masked by paint and with joints (knees, hips,
shoulders, and sometimes wrists) marked by
paint; and those completely painted. Both
types are photographic in basis, and in their
postmodernist mix of photograph and paint
they show that today neither means is privileged over the other. In Appel's sculptures they

structure a dynamic ambivalence. There is clearly an erotic import to the female nudes, but it is largely a surface import. It is the dismemberment and conversion of the figures into savages by their "war paint" that gives the figures their depth of meaning. As savages, they are more threatening than alluring—more nightmarish than seductive. The promise of sexual paradise their nakedness leads us to expect is contradicted by their hideousness. The completely painted nudes—their nakedness is effectively cancelled by the paint—have lost even this glimmer of sexual hope. In a sense, they have been turned into corpses by the paint. One can in fact interpret the two types of works as an ingenious way of articulating the traditional Death and the Maiden theme. In the one kind of work Death and the Maiden have fused—death often appears symbolically as an alluring maiden, in a perfect articulation of Jung's idea of the psyche as determined by the principle of opposition, which allows for one thing to be symbolized by its opposite—and in the other Death is triumphant and undisguised.

This mix of Eros and Thanatos—this unconscious, primitive association of the desire for death with the desire for love (the latter the opposite that masks the former)—appears also in the paintings. Over and over again we see the pairing of biophiliac and necrophiliac colors. Their inseparability is perhaps most noticeable in the figure of Death enthroned in *Bateau de Fous*. It is also transparent in the bull on *The Prairie* and the dog in the *Country*, but in the figure of Death in *Bateau de Fous* it is a more intricate and imminent inseparability. Also, Death, with his cancelled—indeterminate?—genitals, symbolized by the schematic house of life, and his phallic papal tiara, brings one of the key, unresolved issues of these works to the fore: if one finally accepts death unconsciously, what happens to one's sexuality? There is a peculiarly clarified or purified—if not quite spiritualized—quality to the savage handling of all Appel's new works, a special luminosity to them, suggesting the integrity possible simply with the idea, if not the actuality, of the cancellation of sexuality. Psychosexuality, of course, can never be cancelled; one can never escape from or renounce its ambivalences. It appears all the more dramatically and powerfully in Appel's new works—in the concentrated color clashes, in the photography/paint and personal/collective ambivalences.

In fact, hidden in the desire for death which the unconscious recognition and acceptance of death implies—hidden the way the most secret Chinese box is hidden in the more obvious one—is a more deeply unconscious or secret desire: yearning for freedom from the slavery of sexual passion. The aged Sophocles yearned for—but never had—such liberation. But it was through this yearning that he was able to articulate the tragedy sexuality could become for the adult, and always is for the child. Similarly, by making death his purpose, Appel has been able to articulate the tragically sexual coloring of existence. Appel has achieved all that one can expect from a master's late style.

Drawing, 1980

appel 80

Herbert Read

KAREL APPEL
by Herbert Read

Drawing, 1980

Karel Appel was the youngest of the artists chosen to decorate the new headquarters of UNESCO in Paris, which is indicative of the eminence he has reached among the artists of the post-war period. No painter of his generation has made a greater impact on the artistic consciousness of Europe, and the reason is not far to seek. It lies in the power and directness of the images he has created.

Power is a physical concept. Great artists always have this muscular dynamism, this ability to transfuse their materials with bodily energy. The canvas or the stone becomes, as it were, but a momentary trace of the passionate energy that has traversed it. Connect these moments, as in an exhibition, or in this book, and one is then aware of something much bigger and more devastating than a work of art—of a spiritual tornado that has left these evidences of its passage.

Such art is not classical, for it has no measure or containment, no sweetness or rest. It is the agitated art of the Gothic, of the North, which was always preoccupied with movement, with boundless space, with infinity. It was also preoccupied with animal vitality, and certain historical phases of it have been called the Animal Style. I place Appel's art in this tradition. It is an art that has its roots in the frozen soil of Northern Europe—the North of Viking carved dragons, Saxon gargoyles, and those Celtic illuminations where the letter becomes the beast and the beast loses its identity in a thicket of interlaced ornament.

Appel paints animals and also the human mask—the Mask as a symbol of the impassioned and solitary Will, reaching after a superhuman form. I use terms from the writings of a poet of the same tradition, William Butler Yeats, who wrote many interesting things about the Mask and its relation to the Creative Mind. I see Appel's paintings as witnesses to some tremendous inner struggle of the Will with Fate, in which the Will has triumphed over destiny and asserted itself in pure sensation. From this triumph of the Will comes that sense of unity which has characterized Appel's work since the beginning. No contemporary painter has shown more consistency, a more sustained drive towards some kind of ultimate sincerity.

It would be a mistake to write too abstractly about an art that is so direct, so concrete. Appel is not a conceptual artist, un peintre raisonnable. His control of design is as instinctive as a child's (or a savage's). Violent as they are, I do not find terror in his images; as Christian Dotrement has said, he captures the beast but he does not kill it. He then identifies himself with its animal vitality. One must always distinguish between vitality and violence. Though Appel's paintings may be said to stream with the blood of animals, they are not patches from the floor of an abattoir: they represent the physical substance of life itself. Their colors are living, moving, never coagulated or faded. They stream through the field of vision as natural forces, conveying life to hearts that are invisible only because they are hidden within our own breasts.

Drawing, 1980

KAREL APPEL
by Eleanor Flomenhaft

1985

My paintings are strong like life!
Life is filled with tragedy, with the helpless feeling,
Love is feeling, overwhelming feeling and there is
    always tragedy involved with love.
We try to be tough, we try to be nice
But in the end is always tragedy.
The brush stroke begins with nothing and ends
    with nothing
And in between is life
In between is the empty space, the helplessness
we feel in life—the tragic feeling!

Karel Appel is above all a humanist, and regardless of the medium he chooses to explore, his humanism links each stage of his development to the other. Although he views life as inevitably tragic, cynicism has no place in his anima. As Michael Greenwood aptly noted,

> Appel's paintings, like those of Delacroix, express thematically and dynamically the state of conflict that is resolved in the act of creation...the artist's role, as he conceives it, is to fight his way back to a state of grace and in so doing offers mankind an exemplary model of reconciliation with the hidden forces of nature.[2]

During World War II, with the constant threat of the Nazis at his heels, and extremely severe deprivations, Appel and his fellow artists "prowled" the Dutch countryside—barely surviving—exchanging paintings "for a handful of potatoes, a bit of raw herring, or a couple of slices of sausage."[3] For the most part, he painted landscapes in the manner taught him (at age fifteen) by his uncle, and also in the tradition of the Royal Art Academy in Amsterdam which he entered at the outset of the war. One can see in these early works the formulative impulse of Van Gogh's energetic brush strokes which would permeate many of Appel's mature canvases. Although admirably done, they were not merely satisfactory outlets for the enormous feelings provoked in Appel by the sight of the widespread brutal rapacity blighting his country.

Willem Sandberg initiated Appel's face-about. With an eye towards reorganizing the art world in Amsterdam in the aftermath of the war, "Sandberg," said Appel, "brought works of Picasso, Klee and Mondrian to the Stedelijk Museum. He made a big Dada show. And then we saw very clearly that the art from before the war, hard-edge, Surrealism, Dada, was coming back as the new art, and this was not right."[4] At that time, Appel was like a smoldering volcano. He was convinced that possibilities existed for depicting the images imprisoned within him, images which were demanding new forms. Others felt the same way. According to Appel:

Corneille and I were friends throughout the war and then I met Constant. We were all looking for the real new image, fresh and new like a rebirth. We had to learn what came before—the Renaissance, Chinese art, the French art. The luminous feeling captured in Rembrandt's paintings touch the secret of life. Although Van Gogh's canvases are strong with joyous color, you experience in them the tragedy of life. Picasso was a major inspiration for me, also Matisse for color, and from the Dadist, Kurt Schwitters, I was influenced to utilize found objects.

You have to learn it all: then forget it and start again like a child. This is the inner evolution. I speak about it all the time: it is the hardest thing for the artist.[5]

Meeting the *"Host"* group in Copenhagen in 1948, "artists with the same emotional feelings,"[6] irrevocably altered the course of Appel's life. Asger Jorn, on one of his many trips, had already inspired Constant, Appel and Corneille to form the Dutch 'Experimental Group' with the corresponding publication, *Reflex*. But actually seeing evocative Danish art utilizing the enormous potential of folk sources, and encountering people who lived in a spontaneous manner, loosed Appel's feelings totally. Gleefully, he fantasized that, "If I hadn't been a painter, I'd have liked to be a clown."[7] In fact, Appel added that "to paint is to perform without a safety net,"[8] and about Cobra—the alliance which developed a few days before the *"Host"* exhibit in Copenhagen—he declared, "That was my first performance."[9]

In Cobra he was liberated at last. By the time the group dispersed, his canvases exploded with unleashed vitality. In heavy impasto and brilliant colors, Appel conjured up confused beasts, deceptively innocent, ill-proportioned cats, strange birds, pathetic personages and the clowns which would continue to fascinate him. He wrote:

From the mask of what unknown clown
do I derive the faces I paint?
Buried memories of real faces in life:
faces deformed by suffering, laughter, or labor
sometimes mad.
And then they become imaginary.[10]

And art historian, Herbert Read, said of Appel:

He comes from the world of Van Gogh and pursues Van Gogh's final fury into another world, the world Van Gogh was seeking but did not find—the world of abstract expression... Appel takes no notice of public faces... but he represents their private ecstasies. It is an act of internal necessity.[11]

In folk art's countless forms, most Cobra artists found suggestive and experimental outlets linked inextricably to spontaneous expression. As Constant, spokesman for the Dutch Experimentalists, pointed out in *Reflex no. 1*: "Folk art is the manifestation of life fed solely by a natural... search for expression. By recognizing no other norm than expression, folk art is created according to impulse and intuition." Specifically cited was the child who, like primitive creatures, "knows no other law that the spontaneous feeling for life and has no other need than to express this."[12] Appel began his own quest for a new way by focusing on children. He, too, found both the child's innonence as well as his open aggressiveness similar to that of primitive man. He saw children as closest to the origination of life, and their responses most directly related to their environment. Therefore, for Appel, they represented hope and the rebirth which he sought for himself.

Wide-eyed interrogating children, whom he likened to "a nest full of light bulbs"[5] were among Appel's favorite motifs in the early years. In *objetspoubelles* (rubbish objects) assemblages such as *The Questioning Children* (1949; 98), that synthesized the 'found' article as in Dadaist Kurt Schwitters poetic *'merz'* collages with 'found' objects by the Surrealists, he expressed the many dualities that coexist in children. Appropriately he chose his objects as though he were a child retrieving castoff objects from the trash heap for his play.

Appel approached the *Questioning Children* by reaching back to his own feelings of a child in order to tap his primal instincts. The work is a construction of sharply outlined wood pieces nailed to a board and painted over with bright primary colors. The forms are like those a child might use in his own drawings; huge eyes are round as moons, ears on the right-top are simple triangles; outstretched arms resemble the stems on a tree. Markings which surround the face in the upper left corner can be compared with the parallel linework on a child's painting as from a Stedelijk museum exhibit of children's art, illustrated in *Cobra* no. 4. Further, the bold square faces, coarsely wrought, bear marked resemblances to carved faces on objects of primitive cultures that Cobra artists were looking at, and are illustrated in *Cobra* no. 1. In fact, brief slashes of color throughout *The Questioning Children* appear to resemble scarifications on these same primitive masks.

To achieve a raw purity Appel may also have been influenced by Jean Dubuffet. The Amsterdammer had visited Paris in 1947, where he saw Dubuffet's *art brut* paintings encrusted with tar, grit, broken glass and anthracite. In these works Appel surely recognized a primordiality similar to his own ambitions.

In 1949, Appel created a mural for Amsterdam's city hall canteen, which once again he named '*The Questioning Children*.' Covered up after a furor over what was considered the

With Pierre Alechinsky, Paris, 1961.

work's violent character, this act precipitated Appel's departure from Holland. A decade later, as a kind of cachet to his international success, the mural was uncovered, no longer viewed as an impediment to digestion. Perhaps the Dutch had come to appreciate Appel's creation, but more likely they were acknowledging their pride in his professional stature. As it did other members of the Cobra group, Surrealism influenced Appel. In the Cobra years he seems to have integrated automatism, mythopoetic iconography and a primitive use of materials. However, the full blossoming of combined forms with the more compelling ontological concerns appears to have taken place around 1953, after Cobra disbanded. This can be seen, for example, in a work such as *Mother and Child* (1953). The expression of the child—who is as tall as the mother—alternates between *naiveté* and aggression, that of the mother between tenderness and fierceness. Colors are bold: impasto is thick. A tactile gestural abstraction erupts out of an automatic script. In this painting Appel can be seen to fuse primitivistic feelings of his own child world with imagery he considered basic to the human condition.

Appel struggles to put optimism into his

paintings. He has said, "I fight to do that. To paint the greyness of life has no tension; to have strength of life on our planet, you have to fight for it."[13] Indeed, one can often detect in an Appel painting a brave although grotesque gallows-smile flashing across the visage of an isolated figure trying desperately to maintain dignity in a menacing world.

An extrovert, Appel is rooted in the world of reality. His roots are close to the surface, unlike those of Carl-Henning Pedersen, for instance, whose bearings are entrenched in the mythical world of the Norsemen. And, just as trees with shallow roots are more susceptible to the elements, in the same way Appel is more sensitive to his environment. His existential situation affects his total being. Thus his paintings always speak of the human condition, whether in his landscapes, nudes, birds, cats, personages or children, it is his total interaction with the real world, his lack of defenses or defensiveness, which is revealed naked on the canvas.

And, like others of the Cobra clan, he, too, is totally involved with his materials. His point of departure is the matter with which he creates his work. To see this, we have only to study the work *Falling Head With Planet* (1959, 108). The

Drawing, 1980

forms emerge out of depths of matter, which could be paint or perhaps molten lava. The paint has always been his master. He says,

> As I build my concentration, I feel as a servant to the paint. I serve it; there is an energy between us. We work together, the paint, the canvas and me...the motor goes on and the image comes back to me, and I give it back, and it goes like that, back and forth![14]

Particularly in this area, philosopher Gaston Bachelard was admired by the Cobra group. He likened the artist to "an engraver ...whose tool will bring us back to sure matter."[15]

Appel constantly experiments with new forms for his images. Two outstanding examples are the mixed media work—collage, paper and toys on board—entitled *Indian* (1963) and the acrylic and wood assemblage called *The Theater* (1969). Regardless of his tools or the approach, each is part of an externalization of his existential situation. His art at all times results from alternations of excruciating pain, tear-filled laughter and tender ecstasy.

And about color, Appel declares:

> It is for me the shock. People say my color is pure color. Not true. I mix all my colors: my red is mixed with another red, and I add some white to take the black out of red, and then a little yellow to bring

warmth back. Only for the line I use the tube, for a spontaneous line: and I also use the brush, the knife my hand. I take everything, every possible way to make a painting free and loose.[16]

Sometimes mounds of paint are squeezed directly from Appel's paint tube. At other times he layers the paint with a palette knife or lets it drip deep into the crevices of the oily mass. In 1978 he began to apply broad bands to his canvases which once again recall the markings on the masks of primitive cultures.

Another thing [says Appel], I see all the accidents; if they look good, I profit from them and keep them. I follow the accidents; that is what I look for. I see all the accidents together as a painting.[17]

Appel's work has changed markedly since the early Cobra years when his forms and areas of color were confined by heavy black outlines. Those outlines have long since disappeared, colors have been allowed to define themselves and establish their own boundaries. And with maturity, the emotional content of his work has also evolved. According to Appel:

Earlier my canvas was a virtual war, a body in duel with paint...[and] red was clearly blood. With my atomic war finally over red is space. At that time [in the Cobra period] to build up a painting was the most fantastic feeling: little by little I have gone over to a magic space feeling.[18]

–254–

There is no diminution of energy in his more recent works. They have, as always, his own panache; and in his involvement with his material as well as human life they are of a piece with the rest of his *oeuvre*. At times canvases now take on informal shapes; and the figures have a perceptibly different quality from earlier paintings. Perhaps the American on the streets of New York has finally merged with the Amsterdammer.

His treatment of space has noticeably altered since 1956, especially as a result of his first visit to the United States.[19] Working on Long Island, in East Hampton, "His forms [wrote Kenneth Sawyer], though tightly contained within the peripherals of the frame,... broadened into panoramic sweeps of color...[and Appel confessed] he had never experienced such satisfaction from space and light as on the Long Island shore."[20]

America's vibrant youth cult in the '60s reinforced Appel's playful nature. "His little monsters...have grown up into big monsters...and about one (a large metal sculpture) called *Mouse on a Table* (1971)...Appel, always an expert on bogy men, has made a social comment alluding to Mickey Mouse as a menacing bogy monster."[21]

Figuration is an essential ingredient in Appel's paintings. Although he considers the image secondary to the act of painting, it is necessary "because," says Appel, "there is always a figure in the real world."[22] There were times, especially in the '50s, when Appel's works seemed to be devoid of any figurative images, but he shares with the American Abstract Expressionist Willem De Kooning the need to maintain contact with mimetic sources. Appel's *Dansa Amorosa* (1956) and De Kooning's *Merritt Parkway* are excellent examples of their common dependency on images from life. Although apparently Action Paintings at first glance, the titles of both works clearly show the artists firmly tethered to their initial inspirations.

Appel works with facility in a multitude of mediums: he paints in oil and gouache. His ceramics are particularly delightful. He has produced a vast body of lithographic work, sculpts in metals, plastics and olive wood, and he has made films. On several occasions, Appel experimented with the production of musical albums. The first was completed with Phillips Records in Holland in 1961, and for several weeks in 1971, he worked with an independent group called 'Studio 10' in the

North Bay area of San Francisco creating a "multimedia record...sound collage mixing Oriental gongs, a harp, rock band and singer...a new combination of sound paralleling the vivid colors...in his paintings."[23] The album, called the *The Big Ear* after one of his sculptures, was issued in two editions. A limited deluxe edition included an original Appel lithograph.

In 1976, he exhibited a stunning group of tapestries (shown in New York), each containing a minimum of 400,000 silk threads. He had mixed each dye himself—over a period of two years—and personally supervised the weavings which were executed in India.

Despite all these accomplishments in so many media, Appel insists, "I am an oil painter first. I work in every other medium to put distance between myself and the oil painting. A working-out process then takes place."[24]

Appel was awarded the UNESCO prize at the Venice International Biennial in 1954. In 1959, he received the international prize for painting at the Sao Paolo Biennial, and in 1960 the $10,000 Guggenheim International Exhibition first prize. He was the youngest artist to receive this honor, and the first Cobra artist to be exhibited in this country at the Martha

Jackson Gallery in New York.

Manhattan is now Karel Appel's home, "his adopted city." He says, "It's an expressionist city and it gives me the feelings to paint more violent, expressionist art. I respond to the feeling, the people in the streets, all the races together, the sounds, the fight, the struggle."[25] He writes:

City of the world
I smell you. I see you.
I feel you . . .
City where I live among
yellow, red, blue streets
like a multi-colored bird
eternally sparkling with
millions of people.[26]

NOTES

1. Interview with Appel by the author, March 10, 1979. New York City.

2. Michael Greenwood, "Appel: The Romantic Endures," *Arts of Canada*, December 1972, p. 56.

3. "Appel's Circus" as described by Karel Appel to Frederic de Townicki; translated by Kenneth White. Given by the artist to author in March, 1979.

4. Interview with Karel Appel by the author, October 1975. New York.

5. *Ibid.*

6. *Ibid.*

7. "Appel's Circus" *op cit.* [Vol. I; no. 1].

8. *Ibid.* [Vol. II, no. IX].

9. *Ibid.* [Part III, no. 10]. *All The Tenderness In The World.*

10. "Appel's Circus," *op. cit.* [Vol. II, no. XIX].

11. Sir Herbert Read, *Preface in catalog for Galerie Stadler Show of Karel Appel Paintings, 1951-1956.*

12. Constant Niewenhuys, "Manifesto" *Reflex* no. 1 September 1948 [Published in Amsterdam] unpaged.

13. Interview with Karel Appel by the author, October 1975.

14. *Ibid.*

15. Gaston Bachelard, "Notes of a Philosopher for an Engraver," *Cobra no. 6* p.15 [Extracted by the Cobra editors from *Paysage Notes d'Un Philosophe Pour Un Graveur*, Switzerland: Editions Eynard, undated].

16. Interview with Karel Appel, October 1975, op. cit.

17. *Ibid.*

18. "Appel's Appels," Rothmans of Pall Mall, Canada LTD. Catalog for exhibition in museums and galleries from April 21, 1972-July 9, 1973; excerpt from interview by Alan Hanlon, questions by Richard Graburn, p. 18,

19. Appel had visited Jackson Pollock's worshop on Long Island during this first visit to America. He saw a row of paintings executed in the 1940's that revealed a shared impulse to 'Cobra' in Pollock's use of symbols and figuration.

20. Kenneth Sawyer, *Preface to catolog—Karel Appel*, Martha Jackson Gallery, 1960.

21. *Arts Magazine*, September-October 1971, p. 74. Author anon.

22. Interview with Karel Appel, by the author, march 1979.

23. *San Francisco Examiner*, March 15, 1971, p. 43. Author anon.

24. Interview with Karel Appel by the author, March 1979.

25. Interview with Karel Appel by the author, October 1975.

26. Karel Appel, *Manhattan*, poem written by Appel and given to the author in March 1979. New York City.

STREET ART
by Pierre Restany

1982

Painted photograph, 1984

Appel's work is abundant, monumental, and imposing. It spans more than forty years, and that includes forty years of Street Art as well, of walking through cities, collecting found objects, and transforming them into a throng of human figures, an endless gallery of portraits, a fabulous bestiary. The persistence of this metamorphic vision throughout Appel's work is one of the basic elements of the artist's awareness, an intuitive quality of his eye.

Appel says loudly and clearly that he hates repetition, and in his art and life he constantly calls into question everything routine. A stroll for Appel is the perception of difference: the form and nature of junk vary from one city to another. The Amsterdam street is not the Paris street nor the New York street, and the reality of the street in the early 1940s is no longer the reality of the street in the 1980s.

The streets of New York, where he lives for a large part of the year, fascinate him these days:

Without any preconceived ideas, I make myself empty and immerse myself in the whirl of the city streets. Is this a trance? My eye is drawn to a pile of discarded objects. Sometimes I feel extra-lucid, sometimes dreamy. What I discover is what any New Yorker can see in the street: old beds, mattresses, lamps, pieces of magnetic tape, kitchen utensils, advertising throwaways. There are discreet and delicate objects, and others more exuberant and expressive. And just as in Amsterdam right after the war, the street becomes my studio and the place to recharge my batteries. I'm obsessed by the wish to combine all these objects and transform them into a new, sensual, unexpected, unusual, perhaps even truly extraordinary language. I have no rules, but rather a sort of radar. It all runs by itself and things arrange themselves.

There is a great modesty in Appel when he speaks of serious things. He likens his Street Art to a game, to recreation in the midst of re-creation. He is modest because he knows that this game is the very essence of the world. The way he treats a piece of industrial waste, having picked it up at the moment that its functional stage has been exhausted, is to pluck it out of the void of obsolescence and raise it to a new level of poetic expressivity. He humanizes the standard machine-made object that has been used, worn out, thrown away, and lost: the prodigal son returns.

Nearly forty years of Street Art make up an extremely rich body of material. It would be utterly wrong to consider this game with found objects as a minor or marginal effort compared to Appel's painting, sculpture, or graphics, since it is at the heart of the artist's innermost motivations, at the depth of his most spontaneous and profound sensitivity. Street Art reveals the whole pattern of Appel's vision, all the hidden strands in his perceptive web of imagination and feeling. It is an oeuvre within his oeuvre, like a spring that lies coiled beneath the other, often more spectacular achievements. Street Art takes on by turns the look of an intimate diary, a poetry workshop, a bewildering fund of humor, the sociological review of a civilization.

It all began in Amsterdam, where Karel Appel was born in 1921. It was there that he studied from 1940 to 1943 at the Royal Academy of Fine Arts and there that he had his first one-man show, in 1946. "I was born in Amsterdam near the market—the market is the life of the city." Appel knows many markets in the world, beginning with the largest one, New York City. He loves to go to the flea market in Paris or to return to the neighborhood markets that he once frequented assiduously, such as the rue de Buci or the rue Daguerre. He loves the suks and bazaars of the East, and the Place Djemaa-el-Fnâ in Marrakech. But Am-

Gouache, 1952, ink on paper

sterdam was Street Art's first field of action.

Only a few examples of Appel's work from the early 1940s still exist and these mended rags, charred papers, and rusted nails evoke penury and misery. Then, in 1947, his production started to become more regular and more abundant. All of his assemblages of that year are from Amsterdam, and they trace a certain profile of the urban landscape, a certain specificity of its rubbish. Wood, electric wires, pieces of cardboard and cork, string, and old nails abound; there is even a collage of bicycle parts. The works generally take the form of objects mounted on painted wooden panels. Sometimes they achieve considerable complexity, as in the case of a cardboard triptych padded with horsehair or in the red and white *Wild Firemen* made of wood, iron wire, red hooks, and the black tube of a vacuum cleaner, mounted on a metal camera tripod painted white. *Hot Temper in a Loft* represents an "action" in a loft, evoked by an assemblage of hooks, cork, and nails set into a wood door from a seventeenth-century warehouse. (When the early settlers transplanted Dutch architecture to New York, they established the tradition of large, unbroken, functional spaces, the famous lofts that were long used as factories or storerooms before becoming the archetype for the artist's studio. Before even imagining that he would have a loft in New York, Appel had found the door for it in Amsterdam!)

This whole series of junk works of 1947 is marked by two tendencies that were to have a determining effect on Appel's style of assemblage: the use of wood in relief and the recourse to narrative representation, as in *Spider* or the anthropomorphic *Scream into Space*. The assemblages of 1947 foreshadow the concept of three-dimensional painting that was to be developed first in a series of child figures, *Questioning Children* of 1948. These portraits of anonymous faces in painted wood on wood were executed in five versions, two of which include collages of cloth or rags. Later, in 1949, Appel was to repeat the theme of *Questioning Children* in a wall relief made for the restaurant of the Amsterdam town hall. The jury was won over by the harmony of the colors and the supple structure of the formal composition. The young Appel had tamed his ardor and controlled his temperament, but apparently not enough for the public, which, despite the opinion of the experts, was shocked and rejected the work. For ten years it was to remain hidden under a layer of wallpaper. Deprived of a restaurant, the artist was to have an Appel Bar instead, in the Stedelijk Museum in Amsterdam: Willem Sandberg, the director, commissioned it from his two years later, in 1951.

Appel's assemblages of 1947-50 express the powerful attraction of Dutch urban folklore, the landscape of the Amsterdam street. Amsterdam is not only a market city, but a port city as well. As in Venice, there is water everywhere, and also wood. Hulls of ships and boats, driftwood eroded by seawater, brightly painted doors and windows and fences, smoothly polished floors and furniture. The sailor, the craftsman, the peasant, the bourgeois city dweller—everybody in Holland joins in the worship of wood, the great national passion, from the wooden shoe to the three-masted schooner. Appel succumbed to the potent fascination of this material, omnipresent in the streets, immediately available for metamorphosis, arousing the mind and senses, stimulating dreams and the imagination. With just a few touches of color, the worm-eaten driftwood becomes a mysterious fetish or a dazzling treasure. Painted wood panels abound from this period of Appel's work; they evoke heads, figures, boneless animals, strange silhouettes. In 1947, during his first stay in Paris, in the studio of the sculptor Tajiri, he had no hesitation about picking up pieces of wood in order to compose and paint them. This was still during what Appel calls his "pre-plastic" period in Street Art. He means, of course, the material plastic, which was almost nonexistent in postwar Dutch trash-cans. It was in 1947—and he is not about to forget it—that Appel came upon his first piece of red plastic in the gutter. It had an oddly crumpled look, suggesting a silhouette in motion; it was to become *Walking Figure*.

In 1948 Appel joined Corneille and Constant, his companions in the Dutch group Reflex (founded that same year), in establishing Cobra, a northern movement that crystallized around the radiant personality of the Dane Asger Jorn. Events moved swiftly. In 1950 Appel, Corneille, and Constant settled in Paris, opposite the Halle aux Cuirs, in some tanning storerooms that had been converted into studios. They had gone there to join Jorn, who was sharing a house with Robert Jacobsen on the rue de la Tuilerie in the suburb of Suresnes. It was in Suresnes later that year that Appel executed *The Smile*, his single piece of welded metal sculpture, by gathering up the pieces of scrap metal that Jacobsen had not used in his abstract compositions (*The Smile* curiously anticipates Jacobsen's future series of Dolls).

The year 1950 marked the climax of Cobra's militant action as a group: Appel modeled in painted plaster the piece symbolizing the movement, *Cobra Bird*, which was later to be cast in bronze. The turning point for the movement, which was as important for Appel's destiny as for that of the whole group, came in 1950-51, when Michel Ragon became Cobra's spokesman in Paris. Ragon had gone to Denmark in 1947 with Jean-Michel Atlan, whose harsh Berber forms showed an affinity with the northerners' free expressionism, and there met Jorn and his friends in the Host group (Ejler Bille, Carl-Henning Pedersen, Egill Jacobsen). Ragon was particularly sensitive to the popular and populist dimension of their experiments, and it was the similar neo-folkloric dimension to Cobra that fascinated him. He tried to transplant this element to Paris by organizing, among other things, the first exhibition by the Cobra group at the Librairie 73 in February 1951, followed two months later by a show at the Galerie Pierre.

Appel, whose canvases Ragon had noticed

at Colette Allendy's gallery in 1949 and 1950, took part in the promotional campaign, but his mind was elsewhere, bent on assimilating his Parisian milieu. It was a harsh, sordid, and stinking environment: the bloodstained hides piled up in the Halle aux Cuirs left red traces on the floor as suggestive of a Chaim Soutine painting as anyone might wish. As in Amsterdam, Appel let the street think for him, and absorbed it in a state of extra-lucid osmosis. He explored the rue Mouffetard and brought back the strangest assortment of objects. The junk works of 1950 testify to the exuberance of the quarter and the vital violence of its environment. On the Mouffetard he discovered a number of old box-spring mattresses, and he created two assemblages on metal frames by combining the springs and the painted parts. A heavy piece of rough, dirty wood, which he repainted to suggest a man and his donkey, stimulated his imagination. To this painted wood panel he attached a chain whose other end he embedded in a pail filled with white plaster. *Farmer, Donkey, and Milk Bucket* anticipates by five years the combine paintings created by Robert Rauschenberg.

The presence of plaster in the milk pail testifies to the importance of this material during Appel's Parisian period. After the *Cobra Bird*, he was to execute in 1951 several sculptures in reinforced plaster, cut out and pierced, and painted in black and white with very little color. The most significant piece, *Figure*, represents a silhouette in space that is all white, with light daubs of black and yellow.

Street Art gives us the key to Appel's attitude at this crucial moment in his career. He did many paintings in the free expressionistic style of Cobra: heads, portraits, landscapes, tragic nudes and wounded birds, wild children and imaginary animals. But the expressionism of these images came from other sources and served other goals than the pure and simple evocation, spontaneous and explosive, of the unbridled energy of the North. A stroller in Paris after having been a stroller in Amsterdam, Appel felt himself by instinct to be a stroller in all the cities of the world. He did not feel particularly attached to this or that corner of the earth. Jorn's subtle romantic distinctions between Nordicity and northernism, between Nordic being and northern existence, left him rather cold. Appel's turf was the street, in all its geographical, sociological, and semantic diversity. It is from this diversity that he still draws the electricity for his creation, the ele-

ment that recharges his emotions, that cataly-
zes his imagination.

The 1950s, an important and richly produc-
tive decade in Appel's career, yielded fundamental technical orientations that the artist
would remain faithful to and that would deter-
mine various facets of his work. Following a
pattern that was to become characteristic, his
adoption of a new material was launched by a
specific experience in time and space: Appel
went somewhere, he found something, and out
of it came pure Appel. After driftwood in
Amsterdam and plaster in Paris, it was Ligu-
rian terra-cotta. In 1953 and 1954 he spent two
summers in Albisola on the Italian Riviera,
and there he familiarized himself with the
technique of ceramics.

Resuming an experiment begun in 1947 at a
factory in the Limburg region of Holland
(where he had executed a soberly decorated
table service), during the summer of 1953
Appel did a series of sculptures in terra-cotta
left natural or painted black and white. These
sculptures, variations on the human head, a
theme familiar to him, were exhibited that fall
in Paris at the Galerie Claude-Bernard. The
largest head, consisting of an enormous ball of
clay worked with a crowbar and then fired, was

cast in two examples in polychrome bronze.

The artist has retained vivid memories of Albisola, and he has often used ceramics in his wall reliefs and architectural pieces. From 1960 on, he worked in collaboration with a factory in The Hague, and between that year and 1974 he produced some thirty decorative glazed reliefs involving special color effects and representing the classical range of his visual repertoire: flowers, heads, animals, and faces. Between 1968 and 1974 he created some large plates (twenty inches in diameter) showing animals and archaic faces, some suggesting primitive African and Oceanic masks. After a series of rather abstract figures in relief in 1970, he was to execute his masterpiece in glazed pottery—*Stubborn Elephant* of 1977.

Appel's first ceramic wall composition was executed for a resort in Arnhem built in 1960 by the architect J.J.P. Oud. Eight years later, again with the old master of the De Stijl movement, Appel created for the Congress Building in The Hague two symmetrical wall reliefs on the theme of city people and country people. Large ceramic friezes executed in 1966-67 adorn the façades of two important buildings in Holland.

The one for the School of Economics at

Erasmus University in Rotterdam is an abstract composition of colored forms on a broad white background. For the Shell headquarters in The Hague, Appel conceived a band showing twenty-five huge faces in color.

The 1950s were also the years of Appel's encounter with the architecture of Holland. He was fascinated by the possibilities of realizing monumental projects in collaboration with architects. Commissions for murals soon began flowing in. In 1955, for the E.55 Exposition in Rotterdam, he painted the *Wall of Energy*. It required two months of work on site to execute this thirty-three-foot-long procession of faces and simple forms in primary colors on a white background. In 1956 Appel made new wall paintings for the restaurant in the Stedelijk Museum of Amsterdam and for a school in The Hague. The next year he used stained glass for the first time, illustrating Genesis in six windows for the Community Church in Zaandam, north of Amsterdam. This was the first of an extended series, in which the artist masterfully played with the effects of light and the design of forms and spaces. He made a glass partition for the Amsterdam Savings Bank in 1963 and a glass and concrete relief for the Rotterdam Hofplein Theater in 1968-69. More recently, in 1981, Appel completed a complex installation of stained glass and colored mirrors for the Westeinde Hospital in The Hague.

The 1950s witnessed the worldwide recognition of Karel Appel. Laurels came from almost everywhere: the Unesco Prize at the Venice Biennale in 1954, the Lissone Prize in 1957, the Ljubljana Biennale engraving prize and the grand prize for painting at the São Paulo Bienal in 1959, the Guggenheim Prize in 1960. The 1960s were to be years of hectic exhibitions: one-man shows, group shows, retrospectives in European and American museums. The first full-length books on Appel appeared as well as specialized volumes on his collages and his sculptures.

At the age of forty, Appel had attained the maturity and the fullness of his means. He showed an enormous capacity for work, making gouaches, drawings, and prints in addition to his canvases. The paintings and graphic work were sufficient unto themselves, but not sufficient for Appel. The world stroller had a need for bright sunshine and blue sky, the man of the North had a need for the Mediterranean.

He found time to spend the summers of 1961 and 1962 in Nice at the Abbaye de Roselande, the family estate of Jean Larcade, who was director of the Galerie Rive Droite and had been his Paris dealer since 1955. There Appel executed more than twenty-five sculptures in record time. The miracle, if miracle it was, was the spontaneous encounter of soil and material. Appel discovered the wood of the Nice olive tree: he sensed it, approached it, took its measure, and reshaped it. Willem Sandberg, in a beautiful poem dedicated to the artist, wrote:

> Appel recognized his world
> in the convulsive twist of the olive trees
> Their strength attracted him
> His ax transformed them
> His colors enlivened them
> so as to confide to them his response.

Sandberg captures Appel's creative process perfectly. Twenty years later the artist explained it to me in his own words while we were looking at color slides of the 1961-62 sculptures. Referring in particular to *Portrait*, Appel said: "First I locate the stump, which I choose for its rough form; then I chip it with the ax until the moment when I feel the image spring out from the mass of volumes and whittled contours; once this image has emerged, all I have to do is to establish its identity by painting the wood."

Appel's expressionistic torment flooded on-

With Willem Sandberg, Venice, 1959.

to these twisted, gashed, and torn trunks. The violent stridency of the painting tattoos the wood rather than coloring it. Above, below, in the hollows and on the bumps, white and black are combined with reds, vermilions, and blues. These men of the earth, howling animals, barbaric birds, red dwarfs, white heads, couples and families[1] evoke by the tension of their postures and the brilliance of their colors the ritual pageant of some African or Oceanic tribe. But why look so far afield for a source? Nice is only a stone's throw from the Col de Tende and the Valle delle Meraviglie. What ornaments, what tattoos did our cave-dwelling Celto-Ligurians display when they came to carve the indelible traces of their sacred rituals in the Mediterranean rock?

Since earliest antiquity, from Asia Minor to Spain, in Greece, Rome, Gaul, and Carthage, everything that *could* be said about the olive tree was said, about its origins, its longevity, its symbolism. It is the universal symbol of wisdom and peace, the richness of the harsh, warm earth, the green and silver blazon that unites all Mediterranean cultures. Everything has been said, but Appel has something more to say. From the outset he projected onto the immemorial tree the quintessence of his being, that "dramatic grotesqueness" of which Mattia Moreni has so rightly spoken.[2] He has demystified the ancient fetish, he has restored flesh to the abstract symbol, he has made of these twenty-five gnarled and hacked trunks a striking series of "popular totems." Let no one speak to me any more about "monsters" in this connection! People have spoken too often of monsters in connection with Appel's work: as though the imitation of masks, the use of metaphor and metamorphosis, the manifestations of the poetic imagination in all its vital frenzy were in themselves monstrous, frightening by their incoherence and excess, and hence abnormal. The fantasies to which the painter's imagination gives tangible form are no more abnormal than our own. They are, in fact, the same, and that is why they touch us, move us, and fascinate us: the recognition of this analogical identity is the basis of all visual communication. Appel's carnival spirit is not gratuitous outrage, it is the pure and simple expression of an existential norm. Appearances are never false; they are a momentary facet of the ceaseless change that is Nature. The artist's presence is expressed by the acceleration of change.

Nineteen sixty-three was a European year

for Appel, in which he divided his time between Rome, Paris, and Holland. The production of Street Art was very important, and it was carried out largely in Italy. The works of 1963, generally large, are mostly collages of found objects on canvas. Plastic toys abound, especially musical instruments and artificial flowers. One notes the recurrence of several themes, first of all that of musicians, which constitutes an important series that includes *The Saxophone Player*. This portrait consists of an accumulation of little plastic saxophones, from which emerge a nose (a toy tank with pointed cannon) and a large mouthmade from the keyboard of a typewriter. Reference to landscape constitutes the second notable theme of this baroque kitsch iconography. Two versions of *Reclining Nude as Landscape* show a woman's body (a pile of dolls) with breasts in the form of hills against a blue Mediterranean sky. In another landscape three paintbrushes apply the three primary colors, while a pair of gray rubber gloves emerges to form a voyeur with a camera lens acting as a gaping mouth.

Humorous and popular subjects are central to Appel's imagination. Plastic toys effectively embody this grotesque folklore, in which sabers, horns, and toy machine guns jostle a duchess with accordion lips, a maitre d'hôtel disguised as Groucho Marx, a centauress made of little horses with manes like poodles, a *Lucky Devil* whose hair bristles with bowling pins, and, of course, the inevitable Indians. A subtle collage in gouache on paper shows the profile of an Indian chief cut from gilt paper: a miniature watercolor palette is applied to his cheek, suggesting a tribal tattoo. Graphic elements linked to the technique of collage appear in several other works. *The Bearded Man*, especially characteristic of the ingenuity of this deluxe junk art, consists of a plastic box mounted on canvas, combined with the complex texture of a collage made of cardboard and different kinds of paper (silver foil, wallpaper) to which graphic elements have been added. In the final analysis, it is the Rabelaisian and casual frenzy with which Appel executes these feats of virtuosity that makes him an Arcimboldo of gadgets. He literally juggles with mechanical toys in *The Crazy Mona Lisa* and *The Atomic Hat. Happy Birthday to You* is a good illustration of the meeting of Rabelais and Arcimboldo amid the modern carnival of Street Art. It is the portrait of a baroque lady: the monumental nose is a piece of rubber bordered by flowers; two plastic swans represent the breasts and their turgid areolae; two gun barrels indicate the mouth and two aluminum disks provide the eyes. As for *Eating the Whole World*, it is a dimestore homage to Goya's *Saturn:* a huge, greedy mouth gobbles everything—a regiment of dolls, an orchestra of musical instruments, alphabets of plasticized letters, and even a telephone.

Appel remained on this baroque course throughout the 1960s but he was to soften somewhat the Arcimboldo-Rabelaisian orgy. As early as 1963 he executed in Paris a series of seven portraits that are oil paintings with collages of artificial flowers. The next year he created a delightfully kitsch work, *Woman with Flowers and Butterflies*, whose title speaks for itself. Between 1965 and 1969 he went back to painting wooden panels and executed several series of them. One of the last examples of 1969 is striking for its mysterious appearance, in contrast to the immediate legibility of his popular totems: it is a wood relief framed against a green background from which project a sticky brush and a round face.

In 1965 Appel bought the château of Molesmes on the outskirts of Auxerre, south of Paris—a huge baronial residence with fields and a farm. He restored some vast spaces, which he used for his different studios, and employed as many as seven assistants at a time. From 1965 to 1972, the year when the burden of taxes forced him to get rid of it, the artist spent an average of six months a year at the estate. There he accomplished a huge amount of work in all media, especially reliefs and sculpture. His basic material was plywood, which he cut out and assembled in layers to accentuate the effect of thickness when they were viewed frontally and to isolate the anecdotal details of form. Many of these pieces were padded with layers of expanded polystyrene and painted on both sides with acid greens, strident mauves, blues, vermilions, and yellows—the brightest tones of the artist's favorite spectrum. These relief cutouts began to people Appel's universe with a multitude of grotesque and good-natured giants, with dozens and dozens of figures and heads, often anonymous in their baroque repetitiveness, but singularly characterized, such as *The Man with a Hat Like the Sky* (1966), *Man with Large Mouth* (1967), or *Sun Head* (1966). Giant also were the flora and fauna accompanying the tribe: birds, fish, flowers, and butterflies. Sometimes mounted on a base, sometimes floating freely in space, sometimes attached to background panels to form triptychs, these cutout reliefs constitute a central part of Appel's Molesmes production. Dating from 1968 are several large polychrome sculptures in wood and polystyrene painted in acrylic, including the famous *Maternity*, *Man and Bird*, and *Bird and Flower*. These masterly pieces had been preceded in 1967 by the equally monumental *Big Ear* and *Figure and Flower*.

Appel likes to say that all this creativity started with his neighbor's cow, which was in the habit of coming to graze on his lawn. Since he could not get rid of her, he decided to paint her. *My Neighbor's Cow*, from the beginning of 1966, stands out in white against a red background. Indeed, all of the Molesmes works reflect the same constant preoccupation: the coexistence of man and nature, beast and nature. The artist sees this relationship as balanced, just, and equal: the bird is as large as the man, the butterfly as large as the flower. The sculptures of Molesmes constitute a hymn to life, to peace among the three orders of creation.

"But what on earth can these characters of mine have in their heads?" For a long time the question bothered Appel. In the presence of his countless figures born of wood and polystyrene, and of faces springing from the anonymity of trashcans, Appel feels himself responsible. Between 1969 and 1971 he undertook a series of "psychological relief-portraits"—cutout assemblages of painted wood and canvas. These monumental faces, over six-by-six feet, try to pierce the eternal mystery of life and death. The artist continued this existential meditation in Molesmes, and his gaze fell on those closest to him. First of all, his wife, Machteld, who was the first in a series of portraits. Appel was to paint her twice again, in 1968 and 1971. The 1968 portrait, boldly spirited in its dynamic rendering and heightened by bright colors, is the very image of life. The 1971 portrait, ponderous in shape, evokes by its purplish white tones the sick pallor of a fading complexion. The large eyes, dark hazel with black circles, consume the face, as death had consumed Machteld the year before.

Life, death, there is nothing but movement. Emmanuel Looten, in his preface to the catalog for Appel's exhibition of portraits in Paris in 1956, had quoted a line from the Upanishads: "His world is all movement, governed though it be by a superb union." Twenty-five years later, in a moving poem written in New York, Appel resumes the dialogue and answers implicitly:

Life? I'll tell you
life is a lightbulb
that one day slips out of your hands

and the horizon of the future
is like a jellyfish on the move

nobody knows how far it is
between life and death
mind and spirit
thinking and feeling . . .[3]

But it was time to come back to earth. In 1972, before leaving Molesmes for good, Appel made some forty large cutouts in wood on a white background. Space, landscape, birds, and flying figures here play a primary role. *Back on Earth*, a very free interpretation of a moon rocket, gave its name to the whole series. The 1970s were the years of the artist's return to earth—chiefly to New York, which became the favorite stopover in his circuit of wanderings. Although he had been going back and forth across the Atlantic since the early 1950s, a passionate reunion took place between Appel and New York. He celebrated this reunion in "Manhattan," a poem written in 1976 that is a declaration of love: "City of the world, I sniff you, I see you, I feel you."

The return to the American earth was expressed by an energetic resumption of activity in all fields. Appel discovered new materials, used new techniques. In 1971, at North Haven, Connecticut, he made his first sculptures in painted metal (enameled stainless steel): *The Tulip* and *The Caterpillar*. This new experiment was to find monumental fulfillment in *Anti-Robot with Flower*, a sculpture installed at the University of Dijon. The problems of transporting, positioning, and mounting it were enormous, requiring a special convoy that crossed the whole northern half of France. Appel, who cheerfully followed all the vicissitudes of the operation, remarks today with a happy smile: "What a great scenario for a film!" Between 1971 and 1973, he also conceived some "models for outdoor sculptures." These maquettes of structural elements, such as a column with base and capital in a free style (*Column with Head, Painted Column*; *Two Columns*, were meant to be executed in large dimensions—thirty-three to fifty feet.

New York was above all the world of the street, with its undulating, cosmopolitan crowds, its restlessnes, its traffic, its exuberant wastefulness:

City where I live
in the yellow, red, and blue streets
city like a multicolored bird
ceaselessly glittering
with its millions of inhabitants[4]

In the New York of the 1970s and '80s we are very far from the poverty of Amsterdam during the last world war. The street has changed radically, and with it the whole repertoire of found objects. Appel has talked at length about this subject several times, especially in an interview with Fredéric de Towarnicki. Today the discarded object is the product of advanced technology and the very sign of the civilization that made it. The most anonymous of standard objects—a plastic bottle, for example—illustrates the refinement and complexity of the manufacturing process, starting with the production of the raw material from petroleum and continuing all the way through to the printing of its label. To salvage such an object in order to place it in a new context, that of the poetic imagination, is to withdraw it from its industrial circuit and to turn this product of the machine into an "anti-machine." This rupture with the circuit of technological production is crucial: it is the absolutely indispensable condition for the humanization of the recycling operation. In order to humanize an object, it is necessary to look at it with an unaccustomed and uninhibited eye. It is Appel's conviction that despite the advances of science and technology, man has changed very little. He has remained a naïve creature, conditioned by elementary motivations. Street Art corresponds to these primitive requirements, to the innate need to preserve somewhere within oneself the freshness of childhood. This desire for surprise, for delight, for rapture is expressed by a spontaneous response to the magic of the imagination, by a taste for metamorphosis and celebration.

That is the whole meaning of the Street Art game, Appel's great little game, the catalyst of his vision and motor of his being. He has given himself over to it wholeheartedly since his reunion with America. Taking up an idea that he had already exploited in Paris in 1965, he collected soapboxes to make figures, faces, and laughing heads, while adding brushes, feather dusters, and all sorts of whimsical objects to them. In *Happy Boy* an anecdotal element supplements this array: a clown's head drawn on a plate made of unleavened bread. As part of an advertising campaign for a fast-food place, these edible plates flavored with vanilla, chocolate, or strawberry were offered as free desserts to anyone who purchased the main dish. Such is America—the America of countless gadgets, from lollipops to Mickey Mouse watches, not to mention the soft-drink bottle caps that inspired Appel to make many amusing pieces (*Smiling Girl*) and that are the basis for his Toy Ties, painted neckties docorated with various objects (the first Toy Tie dates from 1974). America is also plastic foam, the cubes of polyurethane that are used to pack household appliances and that pile up at every street corner. In 1975 Appel began regularly employing this extra-light material, which he carves, molds, and paints, giving it the appearance of the solid density of wood or marble.

America is also the mass media, the on-slaught of information, advertising slogans, newspaper headlines. In 1975 Appel created four collages in which he combined headlines to play simultaneously on design and meaning, visual effect and semantic message: *I Know, I Know, What, Do It—Now*. Here is what came out of it:

I know
The machine
That
Prints
Money
World's most sensuous Bedspread!

or again:

Dial your destiny!
Funky
Get me Wet And
Watch Me
Strip!
The
Bi-sexual
Woman

America is also money and sex. These object-collages have a moral, linked to Appel's own realism: in a consumer society, everything is an object of consumption, beginning with information. And feelings, too: objects like feelings, feelings like objects.

When one meets Appel nowadays, in New York, on the Riviera, in Paris, or elsewhere, one is struck by his sense of proportion and his extreme readiness. Readiness in relation to others, to beings, and to things, and, of course, to the world of the street. The game of Street Art is the most constant, the most lucid, the most genuine manifestation of his awareness of being. Since 1978 in Paris and Monaco, he has made several series of painted cardboard boxes that he combines with graphic signs and also of orange crates that he envelops in plastic or wallpaper. These rather discreet and aestheticizing works stem from his thoughts about painting, which remains his *raison d'être*.

Appel has finished with his "circus," as he likes to say. The carnival is over, and he is distancing himself from its creatures. Certainly he does not disown them, just as he does not disown his past. But his awareness of having a past frees and stimulates his imagination. He has rejected what he calls "decadence," that is to say the static comfort of the world of repetition, and is getting ready to be reborn into the world of difference. Everything is possible from now on. The world stroller has caught his second breath in the street. The big city of New York did not disappoint his expectations, and it is as a just man, a happy man, that he pursues the great little game of the wandering imagination. Through the urban stroll and the street game, Karel Appel has opened the secret doors of his mental workshop to the magnetic emanations of rediscovered freedom. What thus operates in him, in silence and simplicity, as though it were something completely natural, is the new revolution of the eye.

NOTES

1. My descriptions are taken from the titles of the sculptures that Appel exhibited at the Galerie Rive Droite in Paris in 1962.

2. Preface by Mattia Moreni to the Appel exhibition at Stadler's. Paris, April-May 1957.

3. "All Kindsa Ways," in Karel Appel, *Océan Blessé*, a collection of poems and drawings, dedicated to Machteld, published in 1982 by Editions Galilée, Paris.

4. In "Manhattan," ibid.

KAREL APPEL
by Vivien Raynor

1986

Nude 2, 1986, 6 × 14′, oil on canvas, (two panels).

Monet lived long enough to see Impressionism demolished but not to experience the revival of his own art—in the 1950's—as a justification for Abstract Expressionism. Being elected the ancestor of a movement on the basis of a surface similarity is a backhanded compliment at best, but it's one that increasingly is being handed out to the living masters as well as the dead—hence the reappearance in Manhattan of Karel Appel, as it were, courtesy of Neo-Expressionism.

Looking on the bright side, such rehabilitations do at least restore to view more or less forgotten artists, and in the case of this painter, who is Dutch, help dispel the fog of art-historical chauvinism. All the same, it's annoying to contemplate the misconceptions that his show at Marisa del Re, 41 East 57th Street, will inevitably promote.

Apart from displays last year at the Anina Nosei and James Goodman Galleries, Appel hasn't been seen here since the early 1970's.

But in Europe and other parts of the world, he has remained consistently visible since rising to fame in the early 50's as a founding member of Cobra. The group, which created its acronym from the names of the cities its founders came from—Copenhagen, Brussels, and Amsterdam—originated in Amsterdam but soon moved to Paris. There, its members—Asger Jorn and Pierre Alechinsky among them—produced what the critic Robert Pincus-Witten has called "a northern version of The Beat."

Postwar automatism, like the automobile, is not easily traced to a single source, although the American pioneers who made it stick usually get most of the credit. Still, it was World War II's stalling of artistic life and propelling the Surrealists to the United States that delayed its development in Europe more than a lack of response to the precedents set by innovators such as Kandinsky. And, if the shows of Abstract Expressionism that began arriving there in the late 40's were a galvanizing force, it was in part because the ground had already been broken by men such as Hans Hartung and Wolfgang Wols.

Nevertheless, Appel has always been bracketed with Willem de Kooning because of his rich pigment and gestural brushstrokes. To many American observers, however, his persistent allusions to reality have made him seem an Abstract Expressionist manqué. Moreover, the painter who remained Dutch has always looked angrier than his Dutch-born American counterpart. And small wonder, for as Sam Hunter brings out in his catalogue essay, Appel and his Cobra colleagues came out of Dada rather than Surrealism, feeling kinship only with the uncivilized, the insane and children, and seeing their own art as a protest against a dying world and as an announcement of a new world.

Today, Appel's paint is more extravagant than ever. His imagery is unambiguously figural and, contradicting the artist's youthful boast of having severed himself from the past, there are moments when he brings Van Gogh to mind. And this isn't because of the windmills he paints, models in terra cotta and in one case assembles out of fruit crates but because of the amazing skill in "drawing" with color. With a loaded brush that is often two or more inches wide, he defines the anatomy of all his shapes, whether they are figures or the spaces in between. Swatches of reds and oranges, lemon and chrome, blues and the occasional apple green, black and white, they hang in an improbable equilibrium.

Sheer expertise separates Appel from most Neo-Expressionists; so does the passion behind his paint and the pleasure he obviously takes in handling it. The fires may be banked—the artist conceded in 1979 that his personal "atomic war" was over and that the red, signifying blood in his Cobra period, now denotes space. Nevertheless, the solitary figure standing with arms outstretched in "The Entry" could pass as a crucifixion, and it is plainly not Eden that the Picassoid Adam and Eve are fleeing in "Before the Catastrophe" but the end of the world. Appel gets shallow and childlike in his smaller compositions, painted on thick hand-made paper and bordered with corrugated cardboard. But strangely, considering a past that includes junk sculptures, Pop cynicism plays no part in his repertory—nor does historicism.

Standing Nude #4, 1987, 100 × 17½", wood, polaroid, rope

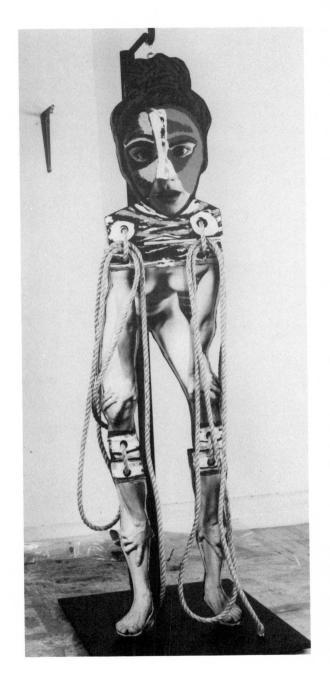

PLAYING WITH APPEL
by Allen Ginsberg

1985

Drawing, 1980, ink on paper

Karel Appel had taken the initiative, old Cobra activist, ten years earlier and written me—we should collaborate. I'd first been in Amsterdam in 1957 and met some of his contemporaries as well as younger poets—Simon Vinkenoog, among the White Bicycle breakthrough poetry revolution energizers of 1953, had known Appel in Paris. Since then I'd visited Amsterdam maybe five times under the patronage of One World Poetry's Ben Posset, and I could find my way on foot from the railroad station to the Cosmos to Leightsplein to MilkVeg to the Amstelside house that Vinkenoog and his wife, Barbara, lived in. They gave us keys so that Peter Orlovsky and Steven Taylor and I could join their family when we visited for poetry singing festivals.

Now the poets we'd met and read with in Amsterdam, Rotterdam, Nijmegen, Groningen, Eindhoven, and elsewhere were visiting the USA ensemble: New York, St. Mark's Poetry Project; Boulder Naropa Institute; and

City Lights Bookstore, San Francisco, on their hejira. Appel came, poet among poets, with Ben Posset and elder Bert Schierbeek—tweeds, pipe, old-dog kind eyes; Jules Deelder—thin, speedy, George Raft black suit, black hair pomaded skull tight; Simon V. and Barbara—fatigued, gazing through my bedroom window at the Front Range at last in Colorado; Remco Campert—sensitive-shy, middle-aged, and wise; Indian Cosmos cosmopolite Hans Plomp in silken orange Shiva scarf; J. Bernlef—inscrutable J. Friday glance; and burly majestic Appel arriving before them—huge vegetarian elephant, healthy because he drank a daily spoon of olive oil to ease off his kidney stones decades ago.

We spent time together at last. Nanao Sakaki, Japanese forest-mountain poet, was visiting; the two recognized the haunted genius look in each other's cold tender eyes. We talked, exchanged books, sang. The day before May Day, Naropa arts faculty's philosopher historian José Arguelles and staff set up a big room full of Masonite and art boards and acrylic in the old classroom where I'd taught International Heroic Twentieth-Century Poetics the summer before. We'd been preparing a Jack Kerouac festival twenty-fifth-anniversary of *On the Road* publication for midsummer and had asked Appel if he could make us a poster image. That became the motif of two paintings. I don't remember the sequence. Karel started the big one with wild colors, "bold strokes," Fauve-Cobra intuitions. But he knew what he was doing—after awhile, the classical image of J.K. appeared rough and ready, gleaming giant, unfinished. Then Karel handed me the brush, to put on words. Now that's where he opened my mind. I had no idea how to hold the brush, what color, where to lay the words. I could think of a few words, but why would he trust me not make a mess of his enormous colored brush-wet visage? "Well, just go ahead—any color you think," he said. "I'm afraid." It's all right, what you make is yours. It's real paint, even if you make mistakes it's okay, we can paint it up funny." So I laid my arm on, climbed a ladder after dipping the brush he gave me into raw acrylic colors laid out on, was it newspaper for a palette? "All yr graves are open"—meaning all Kerouac's buried spontaneities have come back to haunt the world and enlighten it, as in Appel's fearless gesture that made me free to make genius mistake. Then I remembered the original cross airbrushed off Kerouac's breast as it appeared in the *New York Times* and *Mademoiselle* magazine in the original 1956 picture. (It was Gregory Corso's Italian gift, that moment's crucifix; I misremembered San Francisco's Pythagorean aristocrat Philip Lamantia as the poet who handed Jack the cross.) So I asked Karel to paint that in, and labeled it, with a Buddhist AH to cap it off. The giant Kerouac head later occupied center stage during the J.K. festival.

There was still need for a poster image, we thought maybe maybe maybe, so Karel set out again; the smaller collage with Kerouac in plaidlike wool, as I described his shirt—Karel funnily dotted breast and arm to continue the motif out to the wrist holding up a mirror or placard for me to write a poem on; an explanation of Kerouac, Karel asked. So I did that on the spot, twelve long lines in biography of K.'s essential spirit-art, life, and death.

With each succeeding improvised work, Karel left space open for me to make up words and put them in all over, big, right on top of his spaces. Somtimes he'd suggest a color, sometimes a space, other times encourage me to make up my own mind, go ahead. Finally I realized he was actually free of shame and proud to let everything happen, with outside forces marrying and merging into his work, adorned by non-ego, a stranger's words, mine, attentive, mirroring his image, as best we can, I can, rise to the occasion, loose my own mind, no fear, paint the earliest phrases that came into my mind watching his own images splash their way into visibility and coherence, help them cohere even more with my interpretations—freely taking, freely giving. "First thought best thought," as C. Trungpa would write and Kerouac had spoken—permission to be myself, because Karel was manifestly himself and right there solid, a good guy, helpful, big daddy openness, in a free space he'd been living in and painting in for decades since I was a kid, always eating vegetables!

The results you see and can read—funny haikus and mind jumps after the serious concentration of mirror-length Kerouac biography. And Appel welcomed art historian vajrayana Buddhist Jose A. to be artist too and write his own loose-minded words on the acrylic boards.

May Day, after the readings at Naropa and Colorado U., we had a big party with Lama Chogyam Trungpa and all the Dutch and US poets and meditators and yoginis and Vajra guards and Shambhala warriors and Naropa professors and flower arrangers and archery and tea experts, outdoors on a hill house in a garden, beautiful day. There Trungpa Rinpoche's attendants unrolled a giant spread of white paper for calligraphy games—Rinpoche drew a big-tailed awkward small-headed bird, with elegant tailfeather trailing ragged ink. "What's that?' I asked, "Might be a peacock," murmured Rinpoche in his white silk summer suit, sipping sake, left leg clubfoot, his bulk upheld to the calligraphy table by his secretary. Karel Appel looked with a naked slow glance, accepted the brush, and inked in a big black outlined staring empty eye standing up on the left beside the guru's big conscious bird.

All these images were left as gifts for Naropa
when Appel flew to New York.

All Yr Graves are Open
O Jack of Light

Guard the Light

Guard the Heart

Here's your Cross of Tenderness
they kept from Mademoiselle

"Everything Belongs to Me Because I'm Poor"
—Kerouac

APPEL
by Marshall McLuhan

1980

Drawing, 1980, ink on paper

Starting out to write about Karel Appel makes one feel like a mosquito in a nudist colony—one does not know where to begin. He is metaphysician of the playful and the festive, awakening us to the unexplored fun and delights of our lives. His work constantly reminds us of the *Praise of Folly* by his countryman, Desiderius Erasmus. Like Erasmus, Appel puts on a series of fantastic masks, reminding us of the constantly shifting borderline between the hilarious and the serious. The world of play is inseparable from the world of affairs, and Appel's world of play erases the border between child and adult so that the figure-ground relation between them is reciprocal.

Nobody understands better than Appel the mystery of the wheel and the axle. The one cannot exist without the other and the two cannot exist without an interval of play. This interval of play is of the very nature of touch, that is, the resonant interval which is never absent from the work of Karel Appel. Many people have the impression that he uses his finger as a paintbrush. He delights in toys and in painting toys, nostalgically retrieving the primary world of the child. He delights in many of the effects of Rouault and his world of "light through" as in a Gothic window.

In creating a world of the decorative, Appel transforms small figures into an all-embracing ground. His world of masks is a world of archetypes that do not admit of any development or characterization. He has great sophistication of color and plays with the spectrum as a musician plays with a stringed instrument. Appel also reminds us that one cannot have play without order and ground rules. He is like an umpire who, as soon as he blows his whistle, enables the real world to start up again.

One tradition to which Karel Appel belongs is that of the folk carnival, with its quality of belonging to the whole people. With the spread of literacy in the sixteenth century, this cultural phenomenon tended to become impoverished and shallow and was virtually replaced by court masquerades. In large measure, the folk carnival became restricted to the literary genre as in Cervantes and Rabelais, and later Voltaire and Swift, although it survives in its original form as Mardi Gras in New Orleans.

Nobody, however, has done more than Karel Appel to deepen and enrich the spirit of folk carnival in our time.

Long Shall They Live, detail, 1987, 76 × 96″, oil on canvas

SENSUAL MADNESS AS THE LAST REFUGE
by Donald Kuspit

1988

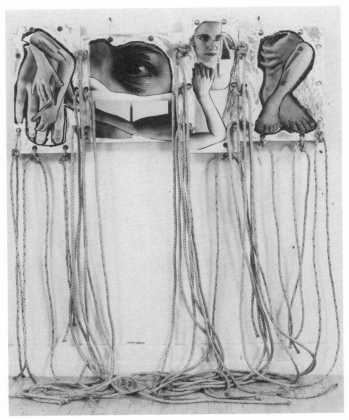

Titan Series #5, 1988, 31 × 69½", mirror, rope, polaroid, acrylic on wood

The great danger today is cynicism, the sense of over-enlightenment, of all-knowingness, which brings with it a new infantile grandiosity and presumption. Our civilization seems to know all that can be known, to have mastered all that can be mastered—except itself, and except human nature, and that is coming too, with the behaviorist technologies (incuding the benefits of the new psychopharmocopia). Our scientific/technological civilization even knows how what is not known can be known, how what is not yet mastered can be mastered: it has set in place the mechanisms for future knowledge and mastery. It has achieved previously unheard of knowledge, a previously unimaginable power of control. It has pushed back the frontiers of understanding—including the understanding of why we do not always understand—so as to create a new sense of the sublime, of the unfathomable. We are perpetually presenting ourselves with the unpresentable, so much so that it is no longer a surprise to be surprised by new advances in knowledge and mastery. Science and technology are our gods, and machines are our miracle-working saints. But after the initial elation at the seemingly infinite prospect of human dominance, there is a strange letdown. The sensitive human being is left with a certain feeling of emptiness: the first sign of the new nothingness, the new disenchantment. Modern enlightenment and power leads the sensitive human being to a new cynicism, which masks an unconscious sense of vulnerability to science and technology, a peculiar feeling of helplessness that seems to resist their helpfulness, a strange passivity that seems immune to their dynamics. Either we succumb to this cynicism, or we begin to wonder anew at what it is to be human, especially in such an enlightened world. Our wonder exists not just for the sake of idle philosophical speculation, but to recover and reconstruct our humanness. It is an effort made against ourselves, for what has happened to us is that we have become subservient to our own instrumentalities, which is why we suffer that depression called cynical enlightenment.

One of the things that remains to be wondered at—if our bodies have not been numbed by our mind turning us into instruments of knowledge and mastery, by our belief in science and technology—is our own sensuality. Sensuality belongs to an earlier epoch in life, to childhood, when it could be unrestrained and groping, site-specific in the body but also generalized throughout its surface. In childhood sensuality is directly available through touch, optimally anywhere on the body. The child's sensuality is not numbed and runs unchanneled through his being, for it is not yet subject to the pressures of the reality principle, not yet directed to worldly purposes, not even embodied in language. To want to recover our childhood sensuality, not only to re-live it but to renew it, to live it as an adult—and one of the reasons we idealize childhood is because our sensuality seemed to run wild then (we forget the restraints put on it from the beginning of life), to exist for itself, to be so open, so openly expressed, that we could feel the lure of its timelessness, seem to enter its eternal spiritedness—is in effect to want to be mad. Yet such madness—the madness of unconstrained sensuality, full of its own delicious urgency—may be our only weapon against cynicism, the numbness of cynicism brought on us by modern enlightened, over-controlling civilization.

The only way we may be able to counter the grandiosity of science and technology, with their absolutization of the reality principle—it is the grandiosity of the adult— is through the grandiosity of unimpeded sensuality, that is, the grandiosity of the child. The risk is of course madness—a regression from which there is no recovery. But art is controlled regression, among other things. Art is a realm of privileged, one might say protected, regression—of legitimatized madness. As Morse Peckham has suggested, since romanticism art has optimally been a zone of allowed chaos, admissable violation of civilized expectations. It is not new to say that the attempt to recover the child's vision has been a longstanding, still ongoing project of modern art, perhaps its major aspect. What is new is to see this as an unconscious attempt to right the psychic balance, to move us away from our decadent overcivilization—and the idolization of science and technology, at the expense of sensuality in particular and humanness in general (its meaning may be problematic, but not the experience of it), is a form of decadence.

The return to sensual madness as a means of recovering our sense of humanness: this is the gist of Karel Appel's art. He not only ventures to make this return, but he is able to make it in an amazingly sustained way, into old age—this is his art's greatness. One cannot help but recall Yeats's remark that he had nothing else but his lust—read sensuality—to keep him alive in old age, but Yeats had spent most of his life repressing it, or expressing it, in dainty civilized poetry, but never really discovering it in full force, until old age released him from any obligations to society and official conceptions of art. It was then that he could experience the altered consciousness of sensuality—that consciousness which is as close as we get to unconsciousness without submitting to or dissolving in it. But Appel, luckily, did not wait upon civilized convention to articulate his sensuality, and did not have an elegant enough youth to forget to experience it then.

Karel Appel is one of the great masters of sensual art—I think that is what it means to be an·expressionist—in the 20th century not only because he dares to articulate sensuality, but because he is constantly searching out new stylistic means to do so. His development has been extraordinarily varied and wide-ranging, involving the utilization of a great number of materials and mediums. He has painted, made sculpture and ceramics, worked with wood, rope, electrical wire, and such found objects as a bicycle and ladder (as in Bicycle Collage and The Broken Ladder (both 1947), as well as the more usual artistic materials. By denying the priority of any one medium he has found the way to greater sensuality. For sensuality is practical wonder at the material—flesh—of being, and each kind of material generates a new sense of sensual wonder.

In a wonderful poem titled "Mad talk," Appel has written:

To be mad is everything
to be everything is mad
not to be mad is everything
to be everything is not mad.

I take this to be Appel's credo: its contradictions argue for the sanity of madness. Its emphasis on being everything seems to me crucial to Appel's sensuality, for sensuality can absorb everything into its own energy. Indeed, Appel has an extraordinary ability to incorporate a variety of materials and objects into his works, with a vigor far beyond that involved in the usual use of collage. For example, in *The Musician* (1963) a variety of plastic musical instruments—and toy guns—are used. A head is in fact constituted by these children's toys. This example of "children's art" is not the usual collage, in which the canvas' flatness is "commented on"—ironically finessed—by the flatness of such materials as newspaper, or in which coarse materials are used to add extra grit to painterly texture, but an extension of the collage to a risky extreme, to vitalizing absurdity. The musical instruments partly mock and partly literalize the modernist idea of so-called "musical painting," but they also make transparently clear one of the major aspects of Appel's work: everything in it madly jumps out at you, tries to grab hold of you, lunges at you—asserts itself in a very forward way. This assertiveness is clearly the point of Appel's dynamic color and gesture, but it is also the point of his numerous figures and heads:. these personages reach out to the spectator like figures in his own dream, sometimes nightmarishly dangerous, but more often with an uncanny familiarity and welcome, an odd sense of intimacy, as though a long lost but unconsciously not forgotten friend. Their confrontational character is not so much aggressive as entangling: their being is strangely like our being, but more fluid, amorphic—more obviously vital. They are themselves, but also, implicitly, our psychic projections.

Appel's earliest work was a kind of street

art, as one called it. *Fishwoman and Rooster* (1947), *The Parade* and *Desert Men* (both 1950), *Square Cat* and *Animals Above the Village* (both 1951), and *The Black Virgin*, *Child with Toy*, and *Street Singer* (all 1952) are important examples of this work, inspired by graffiti but also exemplifying Appel's postwar hunger for life-affirming experience. (Many of the works of this period are totemic in import, suggesting the fetishization of sensuality, of the life impulse itself.) It is crucial to recognize that these were made in the aftermath of the devastation of World War II—and Holland, Appel's native country, suffering in particularly horrific way, if one can say that any country victimized by Nazidom suffered more than any other—and represent a re-assertion, indeed, resurrection, of the life force, if not without acknowledgement of the death wish that forms its inexorable background. Indeed, in all these works the presence of deadly black is almost overwhelming, and in those in which bright color seems more important, it seems forced, deliberately intense—defiantly asserted. The *Fishwoman and Rooster* rise out of the blackness, constituted of the primary colors, as if in refusal of the bleakness of their context. *The Black Virgin*, with her body partially of bright

yellow—her infant son's head is also yellow—
makes the point about the dual of life and
death forces in Appel's work. This has remained a constant factor, Appel always working as though one step ahead of death. In fact,
Appel always incorporates the threat of death
in his works, death not only as literal physical
extinction, but as what the psychoanalyst
Heinz Kohut calls psychological death, loss of
humanness. Such "disintegration anxiety," as
Kohut calls it, is prevalent in Appel's works,
but it is countered by a sensual materialism
that is for him re-integrative. The tension
between anxiety about psychic disintegration
and re-integration through sensuality is the
key to Appel's works.

In *Child With Toy* black death has become the
outline—boundary line—of the red child, as
though to impose limits was to in some way die.
This is another point of the extraordinarily
restless, amorphic look of Appel's figures: they
represent the refusal to be enclosed, and are
themselves peculiarly unlimited. They find
their freedom verging on—risking—formless-
ness. Appel has said that madness means the
absence of laws, boundaries, rules, and represents a breakthough into free feeling, especially free of the burdensome sense of self.

Appel's figures certainly have this extraordinary selflessness. They have, in his words, a pure life feeling, like fish in water.

When Appel came to New York in 1957, it was as though, in its perpetually "unfinished space," as Appel called it, he found the realization of his ideal of the uncontainable emblem of sensual and emotional freedom. He had always lived, as he said, in "small finished countries like Holland," civilized but claustrophobic, their physical limitations seeming to embody sensual and emotional limitations. (And yet an argument can be made that Appel's art articulates, in transfigured abstract form, the same materialistic, life-affirming sensibility of 17th century Dutch art—the Golden Age of Dutch art, when landscape, portrait, and still life were given a more fantastic flesh than they have in reality.) New York gave Appel the license to do what he always wanted to do: "to *paint my paintings unfinished.*" Appel is now a New York street artist, for the street is the space of unfinished life. Paradoxically, it is the place where one can escape from oneself to find one's vital humanness. The street is the place of truly uninhibited sensuality.

The principle of the unfinished is not unfamiliar in the history of art, traditional as well as modern. Implicated in the unfinished is the lyricism of spontaneity and improvisation, indications of unconscious release. In this sense the unfinished is the ideal means of suggesting the full madness of sensuality. This connects with something also inherent in the unfinished, and presented with special intensity in Appel's work: the sense of transience, and what he in conversation has called the "inbetween situation" (which is certainly what transience implies). Freud, in his wonderful little essay "On Transience" (1915), disputed the view "that the transience of what is beautiful involves any loss in its worth." "On the contrary," wrote Freud, "an increase! Transience value is scarcity value in time. Limitation in the value of an enjoyment raises the value of the enjoyment." Appel speaks of his enjoyment of the vital, teeming, adventurous, material life of the streets—his sense of its rich sensual texture. He speaks of enjoying in particular the streets on the edge or boundary of the city, the streets between the city and the country—streets that are transitional between civilization and nature (and thus seem transient), but have their own integrity, their own authenticity. The center of the city is too well-known, he has said, echoing his feeling of oppression by small finished countries. (Appel's complex enjoyment of the streets seems to combine in one sensibility Nietzsche's feeling that the streets are dangerous, revolutionary places; Breton's preference of the street to the museum; Kaprow's celebration of 14th Street in New York as full of more interesting, novel "happenings" than any art gallery; and acknowledgement of the fact that liberation occurs in the streets before it occurs in the home, if it ever does. Appel is always escaping to the streets to transcend the self of the home.) In these special inbetween streets, Appel says, the strangest people—most open, spontaneous, emotionally and sensually free, unencumbered (implicitly, by either the hothouse civilization of the city or the relentless rawness of nature)—flourish. These kind of people are the most human, being neither altogether domesticated nor altogether wild. They are in an inbetween situation, or as I would call it a perilous situation of doubleness, which is the way human beings inherently are. This fundamental doubleness of human life is fraught with transience, for whatever is given in human life—civilized or natural—always suggests its opposite. Nowhere is this feeling of transience more evident than in sensuality, which is all the more beautiful because it is ephemeral and intense. Its inbetweenness conveys the human at its most poignant. The human, Appel has said, is like water that runs out of your hand as you try to hold it, or like a tree that changes appearance every time you see it. The human escapes all efforts to control it, and that ability to escape is its essence. It is this moment of escape into the inbetween situation—the situation of the outskirts of the city, of the ambiguous, porous boundary—that Appel repeatedly articulates in his multi-faceted work, indeed, in part through its multi-facetedness. The street, as he has said, is always an inspiration, because of its spontaneity, variety, sense of the unexpected, and sexuality, that is, mad sensuality.

Appel's style has varied enormously. Being essentially sensual, it can assimilate a variety of other styles into its libidinous fludity, that is, Appel can cathect various stylistic ideas the way he cathects various objects. Thus, he can go to the limits of his collage with his incorporation of such outlandish objects as washboards in *Two Acrobats* (1974) and he can utilize—as in his 1975 collages of newspapers, magazines, and black paper—the Dadaist idea that one needs simply to cut the words out of newspapers and relate them by chance to find one's innermost thoughts. He can produce very flat, unequivocally bright, relatively restrained works, as in a series of 1969-70 pieces and a number of public murals, or he can produce wildly energetic, intimate, more emotionally ambivalent works, as in *Tragic Carnival* (1954) and *Waiting for the Fight* (1976). In the 1980s, in a new surge of creativity, Appel has produced works on a par with his early Cobra works, but more sensually complex than ever. These works are at once more defiant of control and more urgently materialistic than ever. Perhaps more than his other works, they make clear the mythological dimension of Appel's pictorial thinking. A new eschatological dimension makes itself felt in Appel's art. Figures function archypally as well as in terms of immediate feeling. They have a new symbolic as well as emotional force. Moreover, Appel's eighties paintings have a new sensual power and freshness. They absolutize contrast in a way that makes sensuality all the more excruciating. The dramatic method of fragmentation—the eccentric juxtaposition of archetypal image-signs-evident in some of them contributes to this absolutization.

In general, the eighties works convey a sense of breakthrough in intuitive understanding of sensuality, a new level of awareness of its import. Appel's awareness is as spontaneous as ever, but also obsessive and heroic, as it fastens on a difficult idea, a difficult recognition, presented in a vital way. The non-mechanical heightening of contrast is Appel's way of articulating his awareness of the ultimate opposites at the root of sensual ambivalence: the "two fundamental instincts," as Freud called them, of death and life. "The two mingle in the vital process . . . the death instinct is pressed into the service of Eros, especially when it is turned outwards in the form of aggressiveness." "The death instinct . . . can never be absent in any vital process." Appel has reached, and confidently inhabits, this zone of fundamentality, where the opposites of life and death are experienced directly, necessitating a mythopoetic mode of articulation. (Now the full point of his gesture, mingling aggressive and erotic impulses, can be grasped.) This is why, in *The Butterfly of Death* (1984), death appears directly—an allegorical yet sensual figure—in the form of a butterfly, a firm yet poignant form, a symbol of life at its most lyrical and transient. This is why the

Person with a Butterfly (1982)—a ghostly outline of black on a field of white—is surrounded
by a beautiful, abstractly decorative, field of
vitally colored nature, with a sun-yellow dog
(like the baby in *The Black Virgin*). The figure
belongs to the space of death, the rest of the
picture is the space of life, and the dog, half
sun-bright yellow, half black and white, belongs in between, that is, half belongs to nature
and half belongs to its master. In *Man with a
Rooster* (1982) and *Vision* (1982-83) the same
poignant, perfect equilibration of opposites
exists, the same sense of intimate relationship
between the opposites but, after all, their
opposition. Appel has returned to his origins,
but with a new kind of madness: he is on a
different street of life. *Shadows* now appear
explicitly, to allude to the title of a 1981 work.
They are everywhere: *The Trumpeter* and *The
Weightlifter* (both 1986) are stark, impenetrable shadows, as are the components of a *Still
Life* (1986). But there is also light, as a spontaneous gesture, sometimes invading the figure and object, more often surrounding them.
The demiurgic impulse more or less characteristic of Appel's works throughout his long
career is relatively restrained in these pictures, but there is still a sense of forceful

urgency to it, still a sense of intensity. But the pictures as a whole, for all their fragmentariness, are now more obviously composed, as are the figures and other objects. There is, I venture to say, a new gnostic consciousness in Appel, a new sense of the struggle between light and dark. The world is moving into darkness, it is becoming all memory, but there is a light that has detached itself from the world, and seems to exist for itself, on its own, an abstract gesture signaling a new impulse to transcendence—emerging from the core of matter, from the very heart of sensuality. Appel has become a kind of sensual mystic.

STUDIO
New York

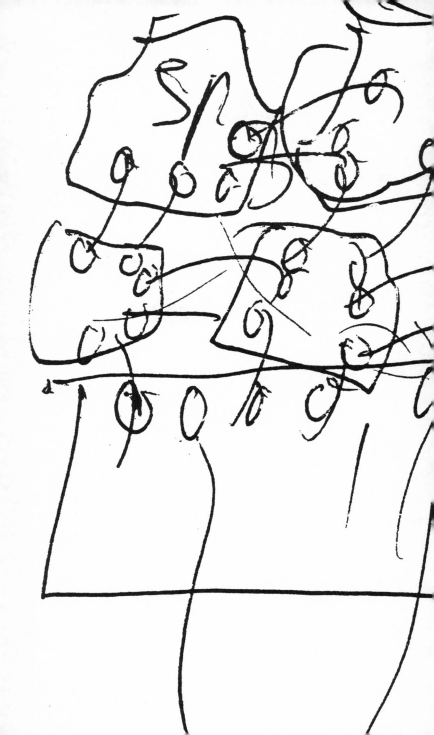

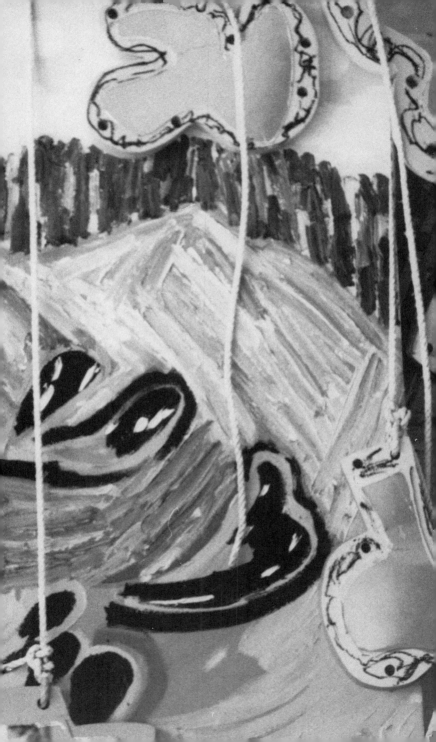

APPEL'S POETRY

DUPE OF BEING

Long shall he live
shall he live long
being long is living
life-long shall he live
shall he live long
live he shall
live long he shall
being alive is living
being alive living is living
long life shall be
living without being long is not living
long life without living is not living
not life-long
not living is short living
short life-long is living long
for life
long is not living
life-long living
living-living life life-long
living life for life
live long life
living short is long

long is living short
living long short
living short long
A short life long is living long
being short is living long for life
short is life
life is short
short as life itself
being short oneself is living
life itself is being short
his life long is short
his short life is long
short life long
long life short
long he shall live
in length he shall live
in the glory of life he shall live long
in the glory of life he shall live gloriously
the rich life
the glorious life
rich as the rich life he shall live in glory
long he shall live in glory
in the glory of life he shall live long
live glorious life to the full
living life to the full is living gloriously
not living it to the full is not living
a life without living
long live life in glory

no life is living endlessly
living life without end is not living
living to the full without life is not living
a life without living not a life
no tangible life
no living face
living with nothing
without nothing there is nothing
life without air
air without life
ashes
life
ashes
nothing
nothing-ashes-nothing
empty-emptiness-life
emptiness nothing
emptiness empty
life
non-existent
life
not living
nothing.
1986.

ODE TO RED

I have known red
I have tasted red
deep in my own red blood
I have known the red of victory
in all its intensity and lust
o, cruel sun of joy
the deep red of sorrow
the torn purplish red of earthly groaning
I raped the red, drunk of it greedily in all its
    hues
down to the veins of my red soul
I was one with the red of the horizon
one with the bloodthirsty earth.

In my inner life exists a desire for the -
    purest red
my nervous system is red
my tissues are red
my entire being is red
the primal animal lies on the beach
as a broken red sun drenched with dark red
    blood

the red of the cry of freedom is the cry of
   freedom
the voice calling for freedom is the sweeping
   cry of red
with all its bonds
the big bang
the red dark distance of the night
the red fields she devours
like a fiery ball
with her hands, her mouth, her whole body.
I hear you, the wind flutters, the morning rises,
the furnace opens, your cheeks flush, eyes
   wide open,
everything grows, everything rages, wild
   turmoil wallows,
fierce red flaring up
like a furious animal filled with desire
explosively, red flares up in me
with a dynamic, impenetrable force
the real essence of red
all of my blood rages red
my whole body plunges into red
with yearning desire red mixes with
my boiling fancy
red has overpowered me.

Red flares up
it roars

running wild, it envelops everything
bloody red breaks the metal claws
and tears the animal's deep red veins
hidden in the immense rocky lairs
the eternal orgasm of fearful phantasy and rage
spewing sperm from the bowels
of the mutilated red earth.

Hideho, keep the blood running
and hideho keep the purplish red running
deep in your vagina, the blue turned red
murderous rape
is torn apart, runs over,
over the soft flesh of her thighs.

Bloodthirsty dynamic
deepest red overwhelms my veins
because the satanic animal drinks red
stronger than blood, fiercer than than the
    sun's red
because insane red makes horny the blood
    of bodies,
becomes the slave of the red blood,
because the red fever devours love
like an axe's blow.

All this is of the past
red lights in old canalside houses

Drawing, 1980, ink on paper

o, red lips with tears in blue eyes
gripped by rough hands
through the snowy windows there was the
     sound
of horny groaning in pleasure
by one tormented needlessly.

I force the red one more time
forcing
the red of space
the red of the sun
of the moon
of the day
getting drunk, screaming, yelling
red red red

painting the landscape red
the trees red
the sky red
the water red
Van Gogh's whirling red
Matisse's red
Rothko's mystic red
Soutine's anguished red
because the painter's red
belongs to the frenzy, the fury
the cruelty
the carnal fear of red

the painter's orgasm of
non-eternal being.

S. Michele di Pagana, Italy
August 20, 1988

FATA MORGANA

Never heard the sound of her voice
floating over the desert
full of space, nostalgia and loneliness
where yellow camels
stare into infinity

and yet I've listened to it
floating over that white burning desert
where the camels
slowly wind across the sands

with dreaming eyes

"I am your guide
to the ultimate and infinite truth
I am your heart
I am your God
I am your child
I am your life
I am your emptiness"

on that hill top
full of space and sky
where tears and happiness come together
I find you again
a transparent crystal
my possible love

MANHATTAN

City of the world
I smell you, I see you,
I feel you. You, city of the
world, city of life
where the steelblue sky
and the ocean touch
and you lie between
like a great inhuman seagull
your big jutting beak
cleaving the steelblue sky and water
like a lance.

Always ready to fly away
into the naked sky with all your
bright neon colors on your
belly and children
astride your big back
ready to fly away, far away
with wings spread wide

City where I live
among yellow, red and blue streets
city like a multicolored bird
eternally sparkling with
millions of people.

Drawing, 1980, ink on paper

THE MECHANICAL IMPRESSIONIST

Close together winter and summer
close together fall and leaves
close together rain and snow
close together rain and flowers
close together lake and sky
close together skin and skin
close together tears and face
close together love and live
close together cloud and sound
close together his trumpet and lips
close together his eyes and his sweat
close together his hands his rhythm
close together his ears and his friends

Drawing, 1962, ink on paper

WAITING-ROOM IS HER NAME

Waiting-room is her name
I don't want to go in right now
I'm feeling great

a crocodile passed by today
I said hello, he said hello
that annoyed me

that crocodile was beautiful
more beautiful than waiting-room

the crocodile says hello
yawns
and goes to sleep

nobody else gets a wink of sleep
only that damned crocodile

MAN UNDRESSED

Waking up
Hands reaching out
Black sky
Rocks trembling
No wind

The fire is dead
The flame no longer catches fire
The cold chills
Weighty leaves
like lead by the rain
immovable by the ice

white is the white of the land
as a shape, limp, she was lying there
in the white whiteness of the land
monumental
fragile
big body
powerless in the white landscape
breathless in absolute silence.

Drawing, 1984, ink on paper

COPENHAGEN HARBOR

The master has spoken
animal head, huge eye
staring you in the face

fight the sun
drink the rain
the sea's gone berserk

Wotan talking

when the giant
wags his tongue
the boats go
up and down
up and down
up and down

the mountains look on
with a thousand eyes
drowned in aqua vitae

Drawing, 1980, ink on paper

MAD TALK

Mad is mad
madmen are mad
to be mad is everything
to be everything is mad
not to be mad is everything
to be everything is not mad
to be nothing is to be mad
to be mad is nothing
everything is mad
mad is everything
because everything is mad
yet everything is mad
and not to be mad is to be mad
nothing is mad after all
non-madmen are mad
madmen are not mad
mad is mad
mad mad mad

Drawing, 1952, ink on paper

WOUNDED OCEAN

Wounded water
deep wailing water
deep red water

the ocean is wounded
like an iceberg
running with blood

the ocean is wounded
the ocean is wounded

the voice of the ocean
will never come back
never
come back

who killed the whale?

On the Warpath, 1984, 55 × 85″, acrylic, oilstick on paper,
mounted on cardboard

THE CRYSTAL WINDOW

I know nostalgia, nostalgia for faraway cities
for the baby of San Francisco

I know the nostalgia of the oceans
the oceans with their strange world staring
their petrified longing

I know nostalgia for loves past
nostalgia for the primitive love of women
the past of the seas
the grains of sand
the eternal lovemaking of tides and beaches

I know the nostalgia of the drum
the voice of Sara
the sounds of the flute washing over her thighs
the blue powder laid on under the heavy
    horizon
a gray nostalgia full of emptiness
the foghorn
the quay
the cranes
the rough voices
the dancing glasses

broads in lace
the cobblestone streets

I know the nostalgia of lost desire
bygone youth
the passing shadow
passion in the attic
birds calling the sun
buds becoming flowers

I know the nostalgia of the sweet trumpet
the sounds of Bix Beiderbecke
the perfume of Harlem at night
the bottles of despair in Greenwich Village
the chest full of hoarse cries

I have nostalgia for a radar
a seismograph
desire for a rocket
that would become one with space
with nothing

I know the nostalgia of our short stay on earth
the nostalgia of children crying
and women's pain

I know the nostalgia of the hidden desire
the fear full of stone-weighted sorrow
the nostalgia of the broken gathering

fragments of stone bits of iron

steel bars all wailing
walls sighing
fragments fragmenting
unleashed liquid gushing through the mesh
everything breaking and broken in pieces
splinters flying
general eruption and explosion

Drawing, 1980, ink on paper

Drawing, 1980, ink on paper

THE HUNGER WINTER

I wish I was a bird
and could fly over fields
where no farmers sowed
where no horses ploughed
where nobody sighed in army camps—
just birds flying free

I wish I was a bird
not the rabbit I ate
when I was hungry

when the people put on uniforms
they weren't people any more
they had no faces any more
but the birds still flew free
the crow and the blackbird

I wish I was a bird

SENTIMENTAL SAXOPHONE

Your old saxophone heart
is flying, full of melodies
over the nostalgic mountains

your lips
like white apples
are asking for pleasure

panic and unhappiness
lie low
in the maelstrom of your mind

getting home and seeing
the faces of the stars
change the landscape into
a huge lumbering crocodile

way up on the yellow hills
the saxophone plays
the sounds of a sentimental ocean
and the tide goes out

birds fly by crying
and their tears
turn into clouds

tired hunting up the past
the tourist is now asking around
for the prophet with the golden pig

MORNING WIND AND DAWN

I saw the light fade
I saw a boat in the sky
I saw dawn in the street
I saw a hand fly away
I saw a rock talking to me
I saw the sun kissing God
I saw hamburgers in springtime
I saw shadows passing by
I saw the tide coming in
I saw lovely ice cream colors
I saw your dream coming back

I was alone, all alone

AMSTERDAM

City of the east and the west
I always see you in my memories
city of bazaars and ships
and harbors and oceans, city of cranes
and pubs, of canals and smells
laid out low behind the wild
dunes of the sea.

Hardly rising above the wild waves,
you lie low under the dark heavy sky,
gorged with water, sunk low in the sky
as though held by invisible hands
safe from the engulfing storms
that come over you like some fierce lover.

City of my youth, low and lower than
the sea, girl by its roaring
love for you, old town of my dreams,
white with snow, where I lived on an old canal
with my very first love
narrow streets full of light, full of music
alleys where the beautiful girls
gave their passion like fans

turning in the perfumes of the evening breeze—
magical northern city of
islands, conditioned by sea and sky
mysterious city
the old neighbourhood where I lived
where the dark red light, the red snow
silenced all noise.

The children of pleasure
like heavenly angels against walls
splashed with neon lights
show their beauty full of pink
and lemonyellow colors
to the restless masses passing by—
there I lived with the soft
yellow, blue and rosepink colours and
the nightly quiet of the moonlight:
mystic city between sky and water
I'll never forget you
eastern city of the north
sentimental melodies, waves
of music from the accordion,
homesickness, the quiet beaches
lying there, the city watch.

City there you lie
with your Rembrandtlike light
your Van Gogh potato-eaters

with your questioning children
like a nest of light bulbs
surrounded by water like a
love-crazy horseman
enbracing the city

ONE HOT SUMMER MORNING

Before the fishing boats
were hauled up on the beach
I saw that big fish
hanging above a deck
waiting to die

two big round eyes

he'd wriggle for a bit
then hang still again
at the end of the line
with a hook in his lip
and half way through his brain

the fellow who'd hooked him
didn't give him a thought
just looked complacently at the water
and spat tobacco juice

another fisherman passing by
picked up a knife
and cut off the body of the fish
leaving the head

so the head still hung there
absolutely still
staring with its big round eyes

Drawing, 1950, ink on paper

CITY CHILDHOOD

The day was full of singing
the night was full of misery
you remember it all

let's have a pizza with onions!

or let's take a cab
and get in touch with you
you, naked, you

naked or dressed
amid the throngs of the street
with red neon light
between your naked legs

going home for pleasure
getting soft like clouds
getting crazier and crazier

Drawing, 1983, acrylic, crayon, ink on paper

NAKED DREAMS

Earthquake everywhere
and naked disaster
prowling around
between night and day

the air still
no wind, no sound
I'm not there
she's not there

time naked as air
as the sky, as water
as myself

her breast was always
like the curved wave
falling on the beach

The Last Regard, 1981, 40 × 59½", ink on paper

THE FORGOTTEN ANGELS

We feel nothing
only the light growing
we feel that life
has forgotten her wings

the world has gone
from sleepy space
to a technological penitentiary
with the sound-tape of human rights
babbling on through the night

one smile, one angel smile
might burn the shadows on the roof
and let us see the stars
like flowers

Drawing, 1954, ink on paper

THE SONG OF THE INNER VOICE

Now we'll sing the wild man's song
the song of the wild man
who lives on top of the mountain
and doesn't want to be seen

now let's sing the song
the song without words, and no sound

here we go
(sit still for at least ten minutes)

OK, that's it
the song of the inner voice
the wild man's song

Drawing, 1978, ink on paper

LETTER TO MY STREET PEOPLE

Farewell, my street
farewell my colorful people
farewell
you were my prophet when I was young
and now I say farewell
farewell my lovely little street
farewell my grass of life
farewell my backyard with the white smell of
    daisies
farewell street-singers
I look at the stars
that speak the language of the universe
I look at space
empty space
I see the peaks of mountains
farewell, magic ocean
farewell, white sands
farewell, my love
the familiar smell of your hair
farewell, farewell

RAINWOOD DISCO

The human spirit
pick it up, pick it up
all the humours of the day
pick'em up, pick'em up
all your dreams
pick 'em up

all the mistakes you ever made
pick'em up, pick'em up

your lips will turn blue
like a cloudless sky

your life
like an unpainted canvas
white as the stars

stick around a while
my little butterfly
my little pretty one
your small round feet
walk the heavens

let's finish this song
and go to sleep

goodbye, little dream

Drawing, 1952, ink on paper

TV IN OPEN WINDOW

I saw a knife
like a stroke of lightning
and a storm of blood

I saw a mouth screaming
and a knife dancing
with a happy crime
that's enough
that's OK
it isn't enough
it's not OK

what I like
more and more
and louder and louder
is the sound of the Bear

ALL KINDSA WAYS

Life? I'll tell you
life is a lightbulb
that one day slips out of your hands

and the horizon of the future
is like a jelly-fish on the move

nobody knows how far it is
between life and death
mind and spirit
thinking and feeling
nobody knows

you don't mind any more
If you don't have the sky in your pocket
like a windmill full of summer days

the great thing would be to
just walk away from this planet of ours
up into the sky of love
with a gaudy parrot on your head

as for the skyscrapers
all they want is to see us
standing in the city streets
and staring like bewildered monkeys

I don't care
you don't care
we don't care

ANOTHER RAINY DAY IN HOLLAND

Maybe we'll have lunch

or maybe just imagine
a monkey in blue jeans
with a bottle of gin

I think about the history
of Dutch windmills—
all that water, all that wind
milling round and round

all quiet today

how's your dirty memory
like the look of it?
think it'll turn you into a poet?

I could be a knife
In dark waters
with a pineapple on the side

good news, great news
about the last explosion
It's all illusion

relax, Max, relax

7 o'clock
wet streets
the red of the sunset

everybody's eating raw herring
maybe some day
they'll eat mackerel

I wonder if there ever was a time
before the rain

The Clouds, 1984, 55½ × 84½"

FILM

Painting for the film *Karel Appel's Reality*, 1961

KAREL APPEL'S REALITY
Film and Text by Jan Vrijman

Art is Adam; film, at best, is Eve
(Karel Appel and "his" film)

The idea of making a film about Karel Appel and his work came to me in a flash in 1957. I had gone to see him to ask him to illustrate the jacket of my book, *Kinderbedtijd* [*The Childrens' Bedtime*], which was scheduled to come out in a few months. I hadn't seen Appel for some time, and I found him greatly changed — more serene, more relaxed than ever — but at the same time he hadn't changed at all: 200 pounds of coiled energy. He had just returned from his first trip to America and spoke enthusiastically about his impressions: the frenzied egocentricity of New York, the fantastic rose of Las Vegas set in its artificial desert, the fascination of racing in a Thunderbird down endless and empty six-lane superhighways, the underworld's control over Churches, unions, politics, the art world — everything. Obviously America had handed Appel a mirror, and seeing all his European philosophical clichés suddenly reflected back at him had enabled him to find a new inner vitality. It was visible in the canvases he had painted since his return, even richer in color, substance and expression, more impulsive and more radiant than his earlier ones. It could also be seen in his own appearance: he seemed to have become magnetized and to give off sparks as though charged with static electricity — it was as though he had a creative erection. All this lyricism may put off some sensitive ears, but to anyone who knows Appel — a man who had managed in a few short years to attract the aversion of his fellow countrymen and the admiration of the rest of the world — such language will not seem exaggerated.

My first meeting with Appel occurred shortly after the war, in the *atelier* of a girlfriend on the fourth floor of a building on Amsterdam's Kloveniersburgwal; in those days he painted for anyone who could pay him with a dish of baked beans or stew, a picture per day, a portrait of vivid truth or a little landscape view of the Gooi.[1] (When, in late 1961, it was announced that a film was going to be made about Appel, I was deluged with telephone calls from people inviting me to come see "one of Appel's old works," and it would invariably be one of these famous splitpea-soup portraits or stew-landscapes.) In the days just after the war Appel also began painting very different works for himself, pictures for which no one would have given a crust of bread at the time but for which today's art-lovers would eagerly cough up thousands of florins: superb drawings and gouaches in primary colors ("I usually didn't have enough money to buy oil paints"), carved wooden objects with strong, rhythmic lines (one of these still sits on the desk of Willem Sandberg, the curator of Amsterdam's Stedelijk Museum).

Appel has always given poetic titles to his works: *Beseeching Children, Fear in the Grass, Nocturnal Animals, Springtime Sea, Dwarfs in the Desert.* Appel's primordial quality is poetic meaning linked with a keen romantic imagination that enables him to cast a new, creative eye on things around him and continually to discover in them new values and new truths. And since we are drawing up a list of his qualities, Appel has the rebellious spirit of the generation that grew up during the war, but Appel's spirit, instead of deteriorating into a gratuitous, negative, frustrated violence, has made him into a rebel *with* a cause. His spontaneous and volatile personality is fueled by a strong, healthy egocentricity, an authentically primitive attention to self — self-centeredness in the best sense: the world revolves around me, I am the foremost creature on earth.

Anyone with such a vital nucleus had to have an exceptional life, and Appel has had one, to his own great joy as well as to the great joy of his friends and of anyone who believes that men are put on earth to blossom into marvelous creatures and enhance, by their very presence, the quality of such a vibrant, colorful and creative world — God's Splendid Creation.

This is also the reason why Appel has always disturbed and upset people who look upon God as a *petit bourgeois* and his creation as a kind of Dutch interior governed by cleanliness, good behavior, a tidy and well-tended garden and what will the neighbors say. Thus Appel's first teacher, the Amsterdam painter Verheyen, inveighs against the most famous of his former pupils: "The only thing he has is a great talent for publicity. When he was twenty he spent months wondering whether he should call himself 'Charles Appelle'. . . and no matter what, he'll still end up as just a hick." (Quoted by Simon Vinkenoog.) The same holds true with regard to nearly every Dutch art critic, all of whom have spent the last fifteen years belittling Appel in their articles because of his

Heads, 1952, 27×21 cm., ink on paper

failure to fulfill their notion of what a real artist should be (introverted, ethereal, sensitive). And of the whole pack of unimaginative satraps, minor legislators, city councillors, editors, whose pesterings finally drove him from his country.

For two years I entertained the idea of making a film about him, without really doing anything about it.

In Paris he was just one of the city's sixty thousand painters, and so he was able to work there in peace, experience the classic years of hardships, organize exhibits and try to catch the interest of the picture dealers. In the Rue Santeuil (where the tanneries made an abominable stench), the painters, most of them Dutch, lived in an old factory that was divided up into a number of studios by haphazard plank walls. It soon became an almost legendary place to friends who had remained behind in Holland. Ed van der Elsken, a photographer who also lived in Paris, captured some of the artistic pigsties on film. Vinkenoog, horrified, reported back to Amsterdam that Appel and Corneille, after homeric arguments, had broken up for good — which would have been fairly difficult given that the walls between their respective abodes were nothing but newspaper.

Penniless, not knowing the language and set down amidst tens of thousands of other painters all trying to elbow their way to success (French, Americans, Poles, Russians, Danes, Germans, Iranians, Chinese), Appel went from exhibition to exhibition with his growing collection of works. He already enjoyed the increasingly active support of the curator of Amsterdam's Stedelijk Museum, Willem Sandberg, who had been one of his earliest (1945) supporters and who was becoming one of the international authorities in the field of modern art. In addition, in 1951, Appel managed to win over Michel Tapié, a very influential French art promoter, and to interest him in his talent, in his vibrant and promising personality and in his future potential as an investment. Tapié gave him a prominent place in several important shows in France and elsewhere. Appel often accompanied him in order to boost his paintings and make contacts.

For three years his work was energetically touted, with good catalogues and press invitations, in a series of first-class museums in France, Denmark, Germany, Spain, England, America and Brazil. By the end of 1953 his name was known to art dealers the world over.

His work was selling well, and for the first time in his life he was earning money. He purchased a small house in Montparnasse and left the stinking studio in the Rue Santeuil. In 1954 he received his first important recognition, the UNESCO prize. His ties to the Netherlands grew weaker and soon there was almost no contact at all.

A six-man crew accompanied me to Paris in mid-October 1961 for exterior shooting.

This filming was successful, but now we faced a much more arduous task: filming Appel while painting. From the beginning I had sensed that this would be extremely tricky—all my friends told me it would be impossible. I knew that Appel never allowed anyone in his studio when he was working; even his wife, Machteld, was regarded as an intruder. For him, painting was more than putting brush to canvas with serenity or enthusiasm. It involved a total engagement of his psychic and physical personality, absolute creative possession, like a sex act. In no way an exhibitionist, he could not stand onlookers. Each time we had discussed the film, Appel had reverted to this question: "How are you going to manage it? I can't have anyone around when I'm painting. Can't you make an automatic camera that will work all by itself?" And each time, I would smile understandingly: "Karel, I've found a solution. Don't worry, you'll see." In fact, I hadn't managed to find any satisfactory solution. I had thought of using the "candid camera" solution, a hidden, invisible camera, which had become fashionable in recent avant-garde films. Ivens had used it in his film *La Seine a rencontré Paris* and Godard in the exterior shots of *A bout de souffle (Breathless)*, as had some French, English and Dutch television directors (Leen Timp, for example), the *Free Cinema* directors and, I was told, Bert Haanstra, who had filmed animals and people in Artis, an Amsterdam suburb, for his marvelous short-subject film, *Zoo*. However, I finally rejected that method as being unworkable: even though I might camouflage the camera behind walls or a painting, Appel would still know it was there and it would create a hypocrisy, an ambiguity, that would certainly show up in the film itself and act against my first demand, which was for authenticity.

The method I finally adopted (and which, in spite of the pessimistic predictions of various film-makers, turned out to be entirely satisfactory) was derived from parallel experiments by Jan Strijbos and Ed van der Elsken, two otherwise totally different characters. Strijbos, who filmed birds in their natural habitat, had quickly perceived that it was not the presence of man that frightened his fine feathered friends as much as it was the sudden changes in their own environment. With infinite patience, therefore, he managed to melt into it, so that the creature being observed ended up by totally accepting his presence without being frightened either by him or by the purring of his camera (indeed, it was only when the sound stopped that the bird would panic and fly off). Ed van der Elsken had developed similar techniques with human beings. He had spent the early 1950s obsessively photographing the Saint-Germain-des-Prés existentialists. With his head of abundant blond hair, one eye constantly shut and the other constantly hidden behind the viewfinder of a small camera, he was such a familiar sight that the habitués of the terraces of the Deux Magots, the Flore and the Mabillon cafés scarcely noticed him. He managed to take pictures, totally unnoticed, from as close as a yard away of people flirting, taking drugs, stealing or just staring vacantly into space. All of these pictures form the contents of his first collection, *Love Story in Saint-German-des-Prés*.

I decided to adopt the same procedure in filming Appel at work. But where? His Paris studio was too small to accommodate the film crew, and he would never be able to feel at ease in a regular-sized studio. I therefore decided to create a "natural environment" for him myself, something new, a space that would be neither a real painter's studio nor an actual film studio, but something between the two, a synthetic space.

I paid a visit to Joop Colson, the time-honored leader of the Dutch "Bohemians," who lived in the immense Groeneveld castle near Baarn, and I confided my problem to him. Colson and Alie, his wife, were all for it: "We'll empty the armory (45 feet long and 30 meters wide, with eighteen-foot ceilings) and Appel can work there. He'll have the entire left wing for himself and his wife." The plan worked out perfectly. As soon as we returned from Paris, work began on clearing out and equipping the armory. I had asked Appel to describe for me his notion of the ideal studio, and that vision guided the entire renovation process: a huge easel for unusually large canvases, two large workbenches for mixing oil paints and gouache and a palette on wheels. I discussed with Van der Enden the lighting possibilities and limitations. I was looking for a constant light so that the only variable factor would be the camera. The film we had selected (Eastmancolor) had a low sensitivity (40 ASA) and thus required a great deal of light; I was counting on the fact that once Appel had got used to it he would be able to function under abnormally intense lighting conditions if there were no other light source to compare it with — daylight, for example. And since I wanted to concentrate on the painter and his material, I had the walls painted a dark gray, almost black (when he saw the results, our host, Colson, rebaptized the room the "Mortuary Chapel").

In late November 1961 Karel and Macheld Appel pulled up in a white Jaguar (Appel's sole expensive toy) and moved into Groeneveld castle. Karel was bursting with energy; for months, he had been itching to begin work on a new series of canvases, but I had made him swear not to touch a tube of paint, a palette knife or a brush before arriving at Groeneveld. I was familiar with his periods of creativity, which lasted for weeks, like a kind of seizure, leaving him exhausted and depleted and unable to touch a canvas for months afterward. I was afraid he would exhaust all his pictorial energy before arriving at Groeneveld, that the time we had set aside for filming would fall right in the middle of one of his passive periods and that the camera would have nothing to film but a morose, absent-minded and bored Appel. Now, he was straining at the bit. He inspected the studio we had installed to his specifications, put on his work clothes and his rubber gloves (for Appel, painting is also hard physical labor, and he takes care of his body like a boxer, does not smoke and rarely drinks, and protects his skin from the deleterious effects of paint). He began to make himself at home, testing and trying out the pigments we had had specially mixed for him in the Netherlands, the quality and tension of the stretched canvases, complaining about the lack of rags (we had forgotten to order any) and pacing nervously up and down the studio like a caged bear. Upset and distracted by our presence, he was obviously doing everything he could to put off the fateful moment when he would have to set to work. This went on for one, two, three days, four days that were especially frustrating for me, but I put up with Appel's irritability with feigned good humor, allowing him time to get used to the presence and activities of the film crew that surrounded him. Then came a fifth and a sixth day... the camera had been loaded with film, tests had been made, the lighting was perfect — the only thing lacking was Karel. All I could do was hope that my ambitious project would not end up as just an embarassing joke.

Late on the seventh day, Appel, after having spent the day grumbling that he would never be able to work surrounded by so many people, suddenly asked if it wouldn't be possible to affix a large bolt to the studio door. Somehow, the heavy lock I immediately had installed overcame the last vestiges of his discomfort. That very day he began to paint: relaxed, aggressive, in complete command. Appel's first brushstrokes were witnessed by only three people: Van der Enden, Dickie, his assistant, and me. After the exhausting vigil of recent days, the sight of Appel exploding into pictorial energy had an unforgettable liberating effect on us all. The outside world seemed shut out and vanished, the only space left was the studio in which Appel was attacking a vast white canvas of nearly 27 square feet as if it were some gigantic monster he had to destroy.

The camera followed Appel for two weeks; as the days went by he grew used to the people and objects around him, so that he began to look on us as nothing but accessories — or not

to see us at all. We easily got all of the shots I had planned, and during the last week I even came up with a new kind of shot, one that gave us better pictures of Appel himself. Unhappy with our camera's limited angles of vision, I fabricated a canvas with an opening in its center of a few square fractions of an inch, covered with extremely pure glass. The camera, which was set up behind the canvas, remained invisible to Appel; no one familiar with art history will see anything unusual in painting on a canvas with a hole in the middle of it.

The last interior shots were made in late November: we did an overview of the development of Appel's work over the past 15 years. Thus the weeks in Groeneveld came to an end. For all of us, it had been a reinvigorating, astonishing, inspiring adventure, all thanks to Appel's enthusiasm and creativity.

"Only the spectators and the painter are present." (Fifteen minutes of film)

During the first showing of the working copy for a small group of invited guests, I heard the following remark: "The film will certainly attract a lot of attention, but not so much for its direction as for the way Appel paints."

I would be tempted to consider that as proof that the film had achieved its goal. Nothing is more ridiculous than a film-maker who interposes himself between his subject and his audience. When it is being shown, a film should, in a manner of speaking, step aside; the only confrontation should be between the spectators and — in this case — Appel.

The film on Appel consists of four structural elements: (1) Paris, in the painter's studio; (2) the painter himself, the didactic approach; (3) surrounding reality and (4) the corporeal nature of the pictorial act.

The beginning of the film, calm and seemingly conventional, situates Appel in Paris. The first image is a long shot of a wide street; lightly off centre screen, as if by chance, we see a *cracheur e feu*. He is surrounded by a crowd of gawkers. This artist is apparently the centre of everyone's attention, but the truly important action is going on discreetly in the background, where a wheelbarrow is being loaded with canvases and paint boxes. We decided against cutting here to a close-up of the fire-eater (tempting as it was), in order not to put false emphasis on what is really a secondary element.

This first shot, which is fairly long (it lasts

for 18 and a half seconds) is accompanied by a barker's voice announcing "The world's greatest fire-eater!" The voice can still be heard under the second shot, which concentrates on the barrow, which begins to move off. The third shot shows a large Parisian square filled with people and the barrow crossing it, now only an almost insignficant part of the over-all scene. In the fourth shot we see it going into a courtyard and, in the fifth, it comes to a halt in front of a small house.

We have already captured in just a few images one aspect of Appel's daily life: his neighborhood, Paris. The painter is now clearly situated in our minds. The present shot, number five, creates a transition to another fragment of his life. Rhythmically, functionally, the color of the picture gradually fades each time the "barrowmen" call out the name of the house's occupant *(Monsieur Appel!)*. At the point the film reaches total black and white, the title flashes suddenly onto the screen, accompanied by the furious tumult of Appel's *Poème barbare*. The credits, which are vigorous but calm, intended to be mobile posters, stand out against a colored background while they themselves are black, gray or white, in order to create a clean break and prepare for a surprise, a color shock, which occurs after the last credit, when the screen becomes a white canvas against which suddenly appears, at the left, the painter's arm, smearing on a vivid slash of color with a palette knife. Thus we are brought to the second structural element of the film, the didactic approach of Appel and his work. For the moment, we confine ourselves to showing the "workshop" aspects of the painter's work and to giving some notion of his aesthetic "ideology." In order to approach this in as analytical a manner as possible, eliminating any subjective or emotional factors, the camera is completely static, totally "objective." We observe the painter as if he were a teacher before a class. Indeed, in this section Appel does not paint, he does a demonstration: a "teaching canvas" was specially created for this purpose, allowing the painter to lay out his working methods rationally. (One fascinating detail: following these "didactic" shots, Appel employed the material he had used for his demonstration as the basis for·a particularly successful new picture that is shown later in the film.)

After having made the initial strokes on the canvas, Appel turns to the camera and says: "I begin with my material, oil paint." The camera focuses on the paint and studies it before showing, in a series of shots, how Appel mixes the paint, adds new colors to his palette, applies the paint with palette knife, from the tube, with brushes, and the various ways he uses those different tools (for Appel, the tube is truly a tool); we see how he endows the shapeless mass of paint with a vigorous expression, how he creates details and motifs, how he alters the appearance of his material with his tools or with his fingers, how the canvas progressively gains richness, intensity.

After having exhibited the whole gamut of Appel's technical means, we have a picture of the finished picture — that is, of the "teaching canvas" Appel had worked on earlier: this shot, of course, was taken much later, although it is spliced into the film at this point.

Then we have a brief overview of Appel's career since 1947, a series of forward and backward tracking shots; this concludes with the most recent canvases painted at Groeneveld. The full view of each picture is interrupted by detail shots, fragments of a few square inches that were microphotographed and have been enlarged to cinema-screen dimensions. These detail shots not only have a great richness of color and form but they also reveal the immense changes that occurred during the painter's fifteen-year development. These images are accompanied by a spoken commentary, the only one in the film. The last six shots of this overview show the "decomposition" of a large picture, shown first in its finished state and then, in one-second cuts, reduced to its component parts so that we witness the various stages of its evolution. The last shot is of a plain red surface, which then fades to an entirely different image, a shot of the oldest Parisian Métro sign, one reading "*Entrée*," which is at the Place de la Bastille. This ties in to the third sequence of the film, which consists of thirty short shots; some are of Appel himself, but all the others are of the world in which he lives. It is, of course, the same world in which we all live, but seen through other eyes. A person's world surrounds him like a jungle surrounds a big-game hunter: a foreign environment having no true relationship with him, creating an absurd but powerfully beautiful landscape. In this world, man is no longer at the center, he is a traveller, an onlooker, he observes the world, but the world observes him as well.

Transposing such ideas into cinematographic language calls for a specific aesthetics: no "artistic" camera work, no elegant play of lines or interesting diagonal dynamics, but an authentic photographing, without frills, one suited to the work at hand and sometimes using a very powerful (350 mm) telephoto lens.

In the script this sequence is entitled "In the Real World." In spite of its thirty different shots — filmed in places that were sometimes hundreds of miles apart — it lasts just two minutes; introduced and animated by the sound of Dizzy Gillespie's trumpet, it concludes in a twilight mood, heightened by the views of the painter's studio at night, where the film's final and longest sequence takes place: a documentary look at the physical components of the act of painting.

We now see Appel at work for the second time, and this was one of the scenario's riskiest elements. Would this be a useless and boring repetition of the first views of Appel in the act of painting? Why not bring all the scenes of Appel at work together in one continuous sequence? Risky as it was, the break was necessary in order to realize two totally different intentions. On the one hand, we wanted to give a logical account of the working methods of a modern painter, in general, and of Appel, in particular. On the other hand, we wanted to show as clearly as possible Appel's own personality (if only to explain his success), and thus, by definition, a purely logical approach would have been quite inadequate. In order to gain a perception of the influence of Appel's personality on his work, the spectator had to be allowed to experience it directly, at first hand, and this emotions had to be aroused.

Combining those two goals in a single sequence could have created confusion and clouded our intentions. The logical observation would have been colored by the emotional climate, and vice versa — which is exactly the situation that inevitably occurs in any discussion of Appel and his work.

So the two approaches were carefully separated in the film, and since each of them consists not only of the shots themselves but also presents us with a completely different Appel, the question of repetition became completely invalid.

During the six minutes of the final sequence, the painter is never offscreen; throughout the sequence, we hear his anti-music, his *Musique barbare*, which is neither accompaniment nor background but, rather, a continual presence, an atmosphere that permeates the scenes and gives a third dimension to the image, adding to its form and its color.

From the shadows of the studio Appel's face grows larger on the screen; his eyes are directed at the canvas, the camera follows his movements. On the soundtrack we hear a few chords played discreetly on a conventional organ, parodying the pompous cultural tradition inherent in the phrase "artist's studio." Then, after thirty seconds, the first stroke of Appel's large red palette knife attacks the canvas and as the artist's studio explodes beneath the knife's slashing strokes, the "religious music" also seems to disintegrate.

Calm, concentrated, full of controlled vigor, the painter lays down the underlying form of his large canvas — approximately two and a half by three and a half yards in size; a multicolored ground emerges, a layer of paint but not yet a picture. Gradually, the painter's technique seems to change: "You've got to flush out the expressive strength of your materials," and for several minutes the camera records an event that must convince even the most skeptical viewer. We see a life struggle, exhausting, imperative, in which the painter tests, continually destroys what he does not want, creates new shapes, structures and colors from that destruction that he then accepts or again rejects, in a creative combat that involves not only his head, heart and hands but also — a difference of degree and not of nature — his entire body: creativity incarnate.

Thus the viewer has an authentic, first-hand experience of the intimate creative process of modern painters, which the critic Hans Redeker has so well defined as "the dynamic passionate movement of the act of painting itself in which the creator, while creating, engages himself bodily and as directly as possible."

At the end of this long sequence, the film allows Appel to pursue the completion of his canvas alone: the end has a tone of objectivity, of relativisation. The painting is completed, the painter withdraws; after hours in which nothing existed for him but the of his own creation, he turns away to face the reality of which he himself is merely a part, a fragment. The last shot is of the vast gloomy metropolis in which Appel is only one person among the millions.

Drawing, 1980, ink on paper

ALBUM

Self-portrait, 1942

Karel and Dick Appel.

With poet Emanuel Looten, 1955.

Amsterdam, 1945

Willem Sandberg with portrait by Appel.

With Martha Jackson and Mechteld Appel.

Arriving with Martha Jackson on the Queen Elizabeth in
New York.

Sarah Vaughn

Drawing, ink on paper, 1980.

Miles Davis with portrait in Appel's studio, New York, 1957.

With Dave Brubeck, New York, 1957

With Pinot Gallizio, Nice, 1960.

With Otto Preminger, 1960.

With Shinkichi Tajiri, 1960.

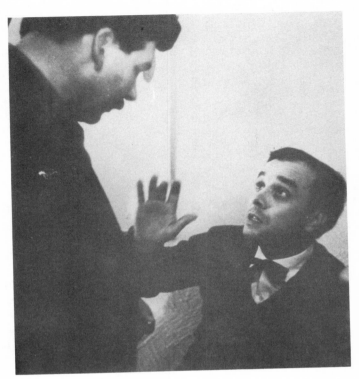

With Yves Klein.

Studio in Nice, 1960.

Book presentation, 1961

With Paulo Marinotti in Venice, 1960.

1961

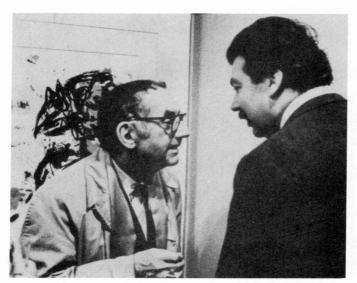

With Man Ray, 1963.

With Martha Jackson, Venice, 1963.

Billy Rose and Willem Sandberg in Noguchi garden,
Jerusalem, ca. 1963.

With architect Jan Rietvelo, Israel, 1965.

With Claes Oldenburg (far left), New York, 1964.

With Alexander Calder.

France, 1965.

Drawing, ink on paper, 1980.

With André Verdet, Saint-Paul-de-Vence.

With Bram van Velde, Paris, 1965.

With Walasse Ting, New York, 1969.

San Francisco, 1971.

India, 1975

With Roland Hagenberg, 1988.

With portraits of Sam Hunter and Marisa del Re, 1988.

With Peter Bellem, Willem Sandberg and Wim Beeren, 1982, Monaco.

With André Verdet, 1986, France.

Painted Mercedes, 1984, with Harriet De Visser.

With Marisa del Re, 1988, New York.

With Min Tanaka, Paris, 1987

With Harriet De Visser, 1988.

China, 1988

OPERA

Peut-on danser le paysage ?
de KAREL. APPEL

Photos of dancers, stage and dressing room if not otherwise indicated by Niko Koster.

From 1935 through 1945 I painted landscapes.

In 1956 I made a painting entitled "Entre la boue et le ciel" (Between mud and sky).

From 1961 through 1965 I worked on the 'mindscape' paintings.

Currently we are in 1987 and after 52 years of 'landscape' I wrote the spectacle "Peut-on danser le paysage?" (Can we dance a landscape?)

The landscape is the sum of the continuously changing interrelations between space, color, music, people, animals, background, sound and light, dance, movement and non-movement.

These elements are in themselves landscapes also, they change forms and colors, just like all of them combined.

The hilly landscape is danced by Min Tanaka, together with cows moving by, with live chickens, with the dancer hanging/moving from a balloon, with the dancers moving like leaves across the stage, with roller skaters scooting by, together with a concert of space-filling music by composer Tao.

All these fragments combined form a whole and contribute to the depiction of the landscape, while the expression of the landscape itself is being danced by Min Tanaka and his troupe.

Peintres à l'Opéra

CARTE BLANCHE A
PAUL JENKINS ET KAREL APPEL

DIRECTION MUSICALE : GILBERT AMY
COSTUMES : OLAF ZOMBECK
ECLAIRAGES : JEAN KALMAN

LE PRISME DU CHAMAN

SPECTACLE CONÇU ET RÉALISÉ PAR PAUL JENKINS

ARGUMENT ET PEINTURES : PAUL JENKINS
MUSIQUE : HENRI DUTILLEUX
(«Métaboles», «Timbres, espace, mouvement»)
MISE EN SCÈNE : SIMONE BENMUSSA
LE CHAMAN : CYRIL ATANASSOFF
LES COULEURS : CHRISTINE CHOLET, ANNE CONSIGNY,
CHARLOTTE MUNCK, OLIVIER PERRIGUEY, PIETRO PIZZUTTI
LES OMBRES : FREDERIC BENTKOWSKI,
DIDIER DESCHAMPS, PIER PAOLO KOSS, SYLVAIN RICHARD

PEUT-ON DANSER LE PAYSAGE ?

SPECTACLE CONÇU ET RÉALISÉ PAR KAREL APPEL

ARGUMENT ET PEINTURES : KAREL APPEL
MUSIQUE : NGUYEN THIEN DAO
(«Giai Phong» et Concerto pour piano)
PIANO SOLO : JEAN-FRANÇOIS HEISSER
CHORÉGRAPHIE : MIN TANAKA

MIN TANAKA, OLIVIER PATEY
ANDRES CORCHERO, FRANK VAN DEVEN, JUAN ANTONIO MORAL

PRIX DES PLACES : 20 A 150 F
SOIRÉES D'ABONNEMENTS : 200 PLACES DISPONIBLES TOUTES CATÉGORIES EN VENTE AUX GUICHETS 14 JOURS A L'AVANC
(*) MARDI 26 MAI : SOIRÉE RÉSERVÉE AUX JEUNESSES MUSICALES DE FRANCE

LA LOCATION GRATUITE PAR CORRESPONDANCE S'ACHÈVE 20 JOURS AVANT LA DATE DE LA REPRÉSENTATION
(ÉCRIRE AU SERVICE LOCATION PAR CORRESPONDANCE, 8 RUE SCRIBE,
LA LOCATION AUX GUICHETS
(GUICHETS OUVERTS TOUS LES

FOR MIN TANAKA

Tiller of the stage
growing body after body
bird movement
triangle bird
fish bird
circle bird
a bird ape
you break space in your hands
leap like the sap
inner expressionist in anguish
destroyer of time

Naked as a virgin
piercing
tearing
discarding the black garment

On the white muscles the skin cracks
I hear the sweat flowing
and tearing the pale flesh

Halting
offering
outdoing the madman
the inner madman
the madman cuts the day each time
crazy against himself
stumbles on his desire

Tiger body
bird body
insect body
anti-human body
anonymous man's body
cloudlike body
fountainlike body
noise-swollen body
someone else's passion body

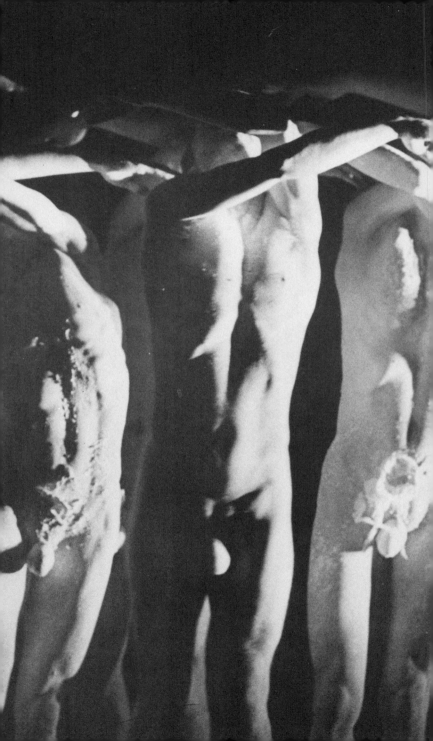

You are black like the flames
of the sun in the night
skin enveloped in black and
white
pale like the movement
of a cloud

Infinity and ashes
savage sweetness
a fire against yourself
expressionist madman flying away full of colors toward the ocean

KAREL APPEL
Paris, 3 May 1987

Min Tanaka

ONE MAN
EXHIBITIONS

1946
Groninque, Beeren Huis

1951
Amsterdam, Kunstzaal Van Lier

1952
Rotterdam, Kunstcentrum Het Venster

1953
La Haye, Kunstzaal Bennevitz
Bruxelles, Palais des Beaux-Arts

1954
Paris, Studio Facchetti (organisée par Michel Tapié)
New York, Martha Jackson Gallery

1955
Paris, Galerie Rive Droite
Amsterdam, Stedelijk Museum
New York, Martha Jackson Gallery

1956
Schiedam, Stedelijk Museum, Hollande
Amsterdam, Stedelijk Museum
Paris, Galerie Rive Droite
Milan, Galleria Dell'Ariete

1957
Paris, Galerie Stadler
Institute of Contemporary Art, Londres
New York, Martha Jackson Gallery
Rome, Galleria La Tartaruga

1958

Cologne, Galerie Anne Abels
Paris, Galerie Claude Bernard (gouaches et
céramiques)
Bruxelles, Palais des Beaux-Arts

1959

Tokyo, Gendai Gallery
Haarlem, Galeria Espace (lithos et gouaches)
Londres, Gimpel Fils Gallery
Zurich, Galerie Lien Hardt

1960

Los Angeles, Esther Robles Gallery
Paris, Galerie Rive Droite
New York, Martha Jackson Gallery
New York, David Anderson Gallery
Chicago, Fairweather-Hardin Gallery
Boston, Nova Gallery
Bergamo, Galleria Lorenzelli

1961

San Francisco, Art Retrospectif Museum
La Haye, Musée Municipal
Milan, Galleria Dell'Ariete
Pasadena, Art Museum (Californie)
Phoenix, Art Museum (Arizona)
Santa Barbara, Art Museum (Californie)
Toronto, Moos Gallery
Washington, Gres Gallery
Los Angeles, Esther Robles Gallery
Amsterdam, Galerie Espace
Rome, Galleria La Medusa
Eindhoven, Van Abbe Museum

1962
Milan, Galleria Dell'Ariete
Londres, Gimpel Fils Gallery
Paris, Galerie Rive Droite (sculptures)
Zurich, Galerie Lienhardt
Seattle Art Museum, Wash, U.S.A. (rétrospectives)
La Yolla, La Yolla Art Museum (rétrospective)

1963
Rome, Galleria La Medusa
Zurich, Gimpel et Hanover Gallery
Paris, Galerie Europe
La Haye, Galerie Nova Spectra

1964
Londres, Gimpel Fils Gallery
New York, Martha Jackson Gallery
Amsterdam, Galerie Krikhaar
Copenhague, American Art Gallery
Esbjerg, Esbjerg Kunstpavillon
Aarhus, Statens Gymnasium

1965
Central Noor-Brabants Museum, Den Bosch
Malmo, Galerie Legen
Goteborg, Konst Hallen
Duren, Leopold Hoesch Museum Der Stadt Duren
Detroit, Donald Morris Gallery

1966
New York, Martha Jackson Gallery
Pans, Galerie Ariel
Copenhague, American Art Gallery

1967

Montreal, Art Gallery
Londres, Redfern Gallery
Amsterdam, Krikhaar Gallery
La Haye, Galerie Nova Spectra
Gand, Galerie Foncke
Exposition de dessins tournante en Allemagne
Exposition rétrospective des peintures 1947-1965:
Amsterdam, Stedelijk Museum;
Bruxelles, Palais des Beaux-Arts; Bochum, Musée
Municipal; Stockholm, Musée d'Art
Moderne; Copenhague, Musée Municipal

1968

Centre National d'Art Contemporain, Paris
Stedelijk Museum, Amsterdam

1969

Kunsthalle, Bâle
Palais des Beaux-Arts, Bruxelles
Martha Jackson Gallery, New York
Gallery Gimpel and Hannover, Zürich
Gallery Gimpel, Londres
Galerie Krikhaar, Amsterdam
Gallery Stephane Janssen, Brussels

1970

Centraal Museum, Utrecht
Galerie La Medusa, Rome
Richard Gray Gallery, Chicago
Galerie Moos, Toronto
Galerie Nova Spectra, La Haye

1971

Galerie Ariel, Paris
Martha Jackson Galerie, New York
Galerie Teatre, Bruxelles
Nantensi Galerie, Tokyo
Kunstgalleri, Aarhus, Danemark
London Art Gallery, Detroit
London Art Gallery, Londres
Galerie Nova Spectra, La Haye
Philadelphia Academy of Fine Arts, Philadelphia
Galleria d'Arte, Rinaldo Rotta, Milan

1972

Rothman's of Pall Mall, Toronto—Traveling
exhibition through Canada

1973

Martha Jackson Gallery, New York
Dalhousie University Art Gallery Halifax
—Nova Scotia
London Public Library and Art Museum,
London-Ontario
Art Gallery of Hamilton, Hamilton-Ontario
New York Cultural Center, New York in association
with the Fairleigh Dickinson University NYC.:
Appel's Appels, a retrospective
Miami Art Center, Miami-Florida

1974

Galerie La Medusa, Rome
Galerie Ariel, Paris
Gimpel & Weitzenhoffer, New York
Gimpel Fils, London
Court Galerie, Copenhague
Gloria Lauria Galerie, Miami-Florida

1975
Gimpel & Weitzenhoffer, New York
Galerie Nova Spectra, La Haye
Aberbach Fine Arts, New York
Wildenstein Gallery, London

1976
Gallery Moos, Toronto
Modern Master Tapestries, New York
Galerie Nova Spectra, La Haye

1977
Museo de Arte Moderno, Mexico City
Hamilton Museum, Hamilton-Ontario (installation de
la section permanente graphique)
Musée 'Slot Zeist', Pays-Bas
Palm Springs Desert Museum, California
Galerie Collection d'Art, Amsterdam

1978
Museo de Bellas Artes, Caracas (retrospective,
déménagée à Bogota)
Moderne Galerie Saarlandmuseum, Saarbrücken
Galerie Nova Spectra, La Haye

1979
Vienna Museum, Vienna
Bonn Musée, Bonn
Janus Galerie, Washington DC

1980
Grace Hokin Galerie, Palm Beach-Florida
Museum Wilhelmshafen, Wilhelmshafen, Allemagne
(retrospective)
Galerie Daniel Templon, Paris (oeuvres nouvelles)

1981

Stedelijk Museum, Amsterdam
Museum of Modern Art, Sao Paolo, Bresil—touring
exhibition to: Museum of Modern Art, Rio de
Janeiro, Bresil
Fondaçao Calouste Gulbenkian, Lisbon, Portugal
Gimpel Fils Gallery, London: paintings from the
1950's and 1960's
Galerie Ariel, Paris
Galerie Nova Spectra, The Hague, Netherlands

1982

Museum Boymans-Van Beuningen, Rotterdam,
Netherlands
Biblioteca Nacional, Madrid
Haags Gemeente Museum, The Hague, Netherlands
Galerie Collection d'Art, Amsterdam
Staatliche Kunsthalle, Baden-Baden, Germany:
works on paper, retrosp.

1983

Fondation Maeght, St. Paul, France: *Appel and
Alechinsky—Encres à deux pinceaux*
Gimpel Weitzenhoffer Gallery, New York
Gimpel Fils Gallery, London
Galerie Daniel Templon, Paris: *Recent work from New
York*
Städtische Galerie, Erlangen, Germany: works on
paper, retrospective.

1984

Palais des Beaux Arts, Brussels
Sonja Henie-Niels Onstad Found., Oslo, Norway:
works on paper, retrospective.
Galerie Collection d'Art, Amsterdam:
"Cobra drawings"
Annina Nosei Gallery, New York: paintings from the
Clouds serie.
Gimpel Weitzenhoffer Gallery: "Personages",
New York
Galerie Ariel, Paris: works on paper
Kunstforeningen, Copenhagen: works on paper
Listasafn Islands, National Gallery of Iceland,
Reykjavik
Galerie Michel Delorme/FIAC in the Grand Palais,
Paris: *Cobra Work*

1985

Palazzo di Medici Riccardi, Florence: a
retrospective
James Goodman Gallery, New York: "cobra
paintings"
Galerie Rudolf Zwirner, Köln, Germany
The Contemporary Art Gallery SEIBU, Tokyo

1986

Marisa del Re Gallery, New York: recent paintings
Arnolfini Gallery, Bristol, England: works from
1981-1985 travelling to The Douglas Hyde Gallery,
Dublin, Ireland.
Virginia Miller Galleries, Miami, Florida
Museum of Art, Fort Lauderdale, Florida
Gallery Rudolf Zwirner at The Forum Art Fair,
Zurich.

1987

Galerie des Ponchettes, Nice France
Musee d'Art Contemporain, Nice, France
Castello di Rivoli, Torino, Italy
Marisa del Re Gallery, New York

1988

Retrospective exhibition at Galerie Beyeler, catalog by Michel Ragon.

Homage à Vincent van Gogh, Foundation Van Gogh, Arles.

Sculpture exhibition, Marisa del Re, Monaco.

ARCO, Madrid.

FIAC, Paris

Artfair Chicago, Marisa del Re Gallery.

Artfair Los Angeles, Marisa del Re Gallery.

Opening of the *Traveling Retrospective Show* through Japan, National Museum of Art, Osaka.

King of the Titans a series of portrait sculptures, Marisa del Re Gallery, New York.

1989

Continuing *Traveling Retrospective Show* through Japan:

The Seibu Museum of Art, Tokyo

Prefectural Museum of Fine Arts, Tochigi

Hiroshima Museum of Contemporary Art, Hiroshima

In preparation: a major retrospetive show in the Haags Gemeente Museum including sculptures, oil paintings, drawings and poetry.

BIOGRAPHY

Copenhagen, 1949

1921
Born April 25 in Amsterdam

1940/43

Studies at the Royal Academy of Fine Arts,
Amsterdam

1946

First one-man exhibition held at the "Beerenhuis" in
Groningen, Holland. Included in the exhibition
"Young Artists" held at the Stedelijk Museum
of Amsterdam. Meets a group of young
Belgian painters.

Questioning Children, 1949, collection Tate Gallery, London

1948

With Constant and Corneille helps to found the Dutch experimental artists' group "Reflex" in Amsterdam which becomes the international "Cobra" group in Paris.

1949

Mural "Questioning Children" commissioned for the cafeteria of the City Hall of Amsterdam to celebrate the publication of "The Call on the Imagination" by architect Aldo van Eyck. After a public uproar and under strong protest by a group of younger artists the City Council orders the mural covered over.

1950

Moves permanently to Paris.

1951

Introduced by Elly Claus to avant-garde art critic Michel Tapié.

1953

First important one-man exhibition at the Palais des Beaux Arts, Brussels.

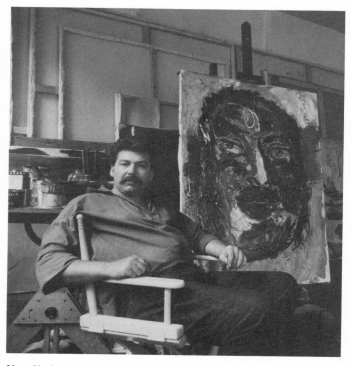

New York, 1957, with portrait of Count Basie

1954

Wins the UNESCO prize at the 27th International Biennale, Venice. Michel Tapié organizes one-man exhibition at Studio Fachetti, Paris. Martha Jackson presents first American one-man exhibition at her new gallery in New York.

1956

Stedelijk Museum of Amsterdam commissions mural for its new restaurant.

1957

First trip to America and Mexico. Wins major prize for nonfigurative painting at "Tenth Pemio Lissone" exhibition, Italy. Wins international prize for graphics at Ljubljana Biennale, Yugoslavia.

1960

Awarded $1,000 first prize among Dutch artists group by Netherlands Committee for Guggenheim International Award. Becomes youngest artist ever to receive $10,000 first prize of the Guggenheim International Award for the painting *Vrouw met struisvogel* (Woman with Ostrich).

Book presentation in Amsterdam, 1961

1961

First color film, made by Jan Vrijman: "The world of Karel Appel"

1962

First important monography published by Harry N. Abrams, Inc.

1966/67
Acquires and substantially renovates the Chateau de Molesmes near Auxerre, France, several large studios.

Molesmes, 1964

With Salvatore Dali, 1963.

1968
Knighted by the Queen of the Netherlands as Knight of Oranje Nassau.

1968/69
Large new sculptures, wall reliefs, and paintings exhibited by four important European museums.

1970
Sixty works from Appel's private collection presented by Centraal Museum of Utrecht. Exhibition catalogue includes major article by Simon Vinkenoog.

1971
In America, series of large-scale sculptures in polychrome aluminum. Color film "Appel Salad" made in Canada.

1971/72
Major retrospective exhibit tours four important museums in Canada and the United States.

Anti-Robot, 1976, Dijon

1973

Tapestry made for the City Hall in Rotterdam,
Holland—12 feet high, 10 feet wide.

1974

Chosen by Allied Arts Commission, California, as
one of three semifinalists for International
Invitational Competition.

1976

Aluminum polychrome statue in the Cite
Universitaire in Dijon, France (33 feet high)
Creates wall murals in shanty towns of Lima, Peru,
together with residents.

1977

18 January: honored member of the Hamilton
Builder Bonnets, Hamilton, Canada.
A donation of the complete graphic collection by
Karel Appel to Geographic Documentation Center,
Hamilton, Ontario, Canada.

Drawing, 1952, ink on paper

1976/78
Creates *Appel Circus*, consisting of thirty
hand-printed color etchings and fifteen hand-painted
wooden sculptures.

1982
Collaborates with Jose Arquelles and Allen Ginsberg
on a series of paintings and poems exhibited in *On
the Road: The Jack Kerouac Exhibit*, Boulder Center
for the Visual Arts, Boulder Colorado.

1983
Begins a series of paintings titled *The Clouds* in
addition to a series of windmill sculptures,
constructed out of terracotta clay and bamboo.

1985
Kenneth White and Karel Appel, porto folio with
prints and poems, published by Francois Benichou,
Paris.
Retrospective exhibition at the Palazzo di Medici
Ricardi, Florence, Italy.
Starting with the Nude series on paper.

1986
Commandeur de L'Ordre des Arts et des Lettres, France

1987
Utilizing life size polaroid photographs, he creates a series of paintings and wood sculptures.
Commissioned by Rudi Fuchs to make a flag sculpture, 10 feet high for Fort Asperen, the Netherlands.
Commissioned by the Paris Opera for the set design of *Can we dance a Landscape?* in collaboration with the dancer Min Tanaka and the composer Dao.
Publication of *40 ans de peinture, sculpture & dessins* Editions Galilée.
Publication of *Nocturne de San Ildefonso* with poems by Octavio Paz and illustrations by Karel Appel.
In November started to paint a series titled *Lang zullen ze Leven . . .in de Gloria*, it consists of 12 paintings each measuring 76 × 96 inches.
One man exhibition in Nice, Contemporary Museum of Art and Galerie des Ponchettes
Summer 1987 makes drawings for poems by Claude Fournet.

1988

Starts *Titan Series* (sculptures made of wood, rope, polaroid, mirrors, and oil paint), *Portrait Sculpture Series* (polaroid, rope, and oilstick on wood), and *Fata Morgana Series* (relief paintings inspired by his recent trip to China).

APPEL
ON
APPEL

China, 1988

When I was small I was very proud of my parents. They were the biggest, richest, fattest in the whole world. My mother was a born actress. But: "If you want to become an actor I'll break your legs!" she often yelled at me. Later she often talked about acting. She would sit in a corner and recite long poems by Multatuli [the Dutch writer Eduard Douwes Dekker, 1820-1887]. She had problems with her memory, couldn't remember where she put things, but those poems she still knew by heart. She knew everything from an earlier time, everything from Proust, Multatuli. Her brother taught me to paint. My mother was a real Amsterdammer, not at all a Dutch type. Her name was Chevalier. I think her origins were French, in the Jordaan [French Protestant quarter of Amsterdam]—long nose, dark hair. Her father was also dark, very quick-tempered. He died young in a fit of passion. After his death, my mother had a hard life— hard work, little money. She went to work when she was seven, cleaning houses along with her mother. Nothing but worries. She met my father when he rented a room from her mother. They got married and started a beauty shop (only hairdressing) in the Dapperbuurt. Aunt Riek, a sister of my father's, looked after us while my mother worked. Aunt Riek loved company, always parties, dancing, lots of fun. On Saturday one did not cook dinner. You just ate the whole evening long pickles and cream puffs. She baked shortbread, coconut cookies, croquettes. And not just two croquettes for each, but plates full. We ate enormously in those days. My mother must have weighed three hundred pounds, just like a fit Italian. She always remained very natural and child-like. She preferred us when we were small. Lots of laughs in those days. My mother had a great sense of humor. She got her jokes first-hand from my father. Even when she was very ill, my mother still laughed a lot. She gave me paint, chalk, and boxes. I have always painted—I gave a lot of thought to it.

From age fifteen to seventeen I worked in the shop with my father. It was a busy shop, ladies' and gents' hairdresser, in a busy part of town. Big outdoor markets, hard work even on Saturdays and then in the evening to the market, lots of fun and music in the streets. Amsterdam bulged with sociability and good food. The laborers were paid in gold ten-guilder pieces in those days.

We slept in on Sundays and then ate. My mother loved companionship and good food. Large tables were set up. The old Amsterdam customs were influenced by the Jewish population; before the war Amsterdam was simply a Jewish town: humor, theater, cabaret, snacks, sandwiches, pastrami, and pickles.

On Sunday afternoons a neighbor came with his car. We all got in, my father with his bowler hat and cigar. "Go slowly," said my father, and we floated through our streets, of which we knew every stone, board, and hole, and my father waved and bowed to all the neighbors sitting on their stoops. "Not so fast!" We went around the corner and stopped again in front of our house.

From the age of sixteen until the outbreak of the war, I did lots of sports, jogging and running on the Olympiaplein. It did me a lot of good.

My uncle in Huizen taught me how to paint. I did landscapes, a little impressionistic, à la Monet.

I always knew I'd become a painter. I also

knew that a son should follow his father's footsteps, and that I did enthusiastically, but it wasn't enough. It didn't suit me; I knew I wanted to paint. It is an urge inside of you, a different feeling, a different view of the world.

Not one of my brothers had stayed with my father in the business. I was there playing hairdresser. I looked outside where life was—the blue sky—and I felt like a bird in a cage. I had to leave, although I loved that people's neighborhood and the life that was lived there. But you know what it is like: always the same, the gossip, the adultery, the indifference. Inside of me there was an urge toward another life, another thought, another world. You cannot escape, and then you have to leave.

I left home at eighteen. My father was sorry to see me go, because I was a good barber. Alone I entered the world of the German occupation. My principal worry during the war was to stay alive while others were starving. During the first war years I attended the Academy of Fine Arts. In order not to be taken off to Germany, I carried an identity card of the Academy. And they had a soup kitchen.

Those years I led a hungry and poor existence; I had no money, and all my friends were dirt poor, too. Cold and hungry and yet working hard—very hard. Crowded Amsterdam became ever more bare and poor and empty, the neighborhood one big misery. Although an epidemic was raging through the world, my beginnings as a painter were enthusiastic. The Academy was a good place to learn about the classics, the Greeks, Romans, and Egypt.

One did live during the war—I lived on the Zwanenburgwal—the Zeedijk neighborhood, the harbor, where all the black marketeers were, where you could trade a painting for goods. The citizens you couldn't sell to; they didn't know you and they hated you. I sang in bars and cafés, and the black marketeers and *nouveau riche* fed me and gave me expensive cigarettes for my efforts.

In those days I also had lots of models in my studio, which was an old attic. Young girls like painters. They think them romantic, and that suited me fine. I had to leave later, was afraid to be picked up by the Germans, and I went with some other painters to the south of Holland, where we roamed among the farmers who had cupboards full of food. We would stay one week with one and three days with another, and we left landscapes here and there.

After the War

Things were even worse after the war. I had spent some time in Twente (the east of the country) and had saved some money, which you had to turn in. I had saved 250 guilders from painting portraits, and got ten back.

I never saw the rest of the money, and of course those ten guilders were quickly gone. There was food for everyone except painters. The poverty was worse than it had been during the war.

Being young, all you thought was, "If only I could have a studio and paint!" That was the hardest thing: to get up in the morning, eat what there was to eat, and start to paint. I did it, but I did not succeed.

I lived in a dirty, dusty studio in the Oude Zijds Voorburgwal. I had stolen some boards, which I put on the floor, and I slept on American cake tins with a mattress over them. No light, very poor. Then the first subsidies came for painters. I remember very well the two civil servants who came to see me in that attic. They were sent by someone, I don't know who. They were taken aback at what they saw. "You most certainly should get a subsidy," they said. "How much?" said I. "Seven guilders a week."

"Fantastic!" I said. "A guilder a day, that's

wonderful!"

"You know what?" they said. "We'll predate your application." In that way, I got fourteen guilders all at once.

1950

Painting is a tangible, sensual experiencing, intensely moved by joy and the tragedy of man.

A spatial experiencing, fed by instinct, becomes a living shape. The atmosphere I inhale and make tangible by my paint is an expression of my era.

1954

Painting is a continuous battle with yourself. The moment man gets outside himself, we can talk about art. I once heard a pianist, and the moment he left the melody and stopped playing, there existed an ecstatic trance, an improvisation, which is the essential condition for vital art. The battle to make hand and shapes, eye and canvas one, a fight between equals. A conclusion that he acts, thus exists. The hopelessness of nonsense. Man has lost courage because of his own nonsense. Hopeless because of the nonsense of society, belief, and love. Hopeless because of the nonsense of the nonsociety. Hopeless over the nonsense to have. Hopeless over the nonsense to have not. Not to be able to have. Not to want to have.

1955

Painting is the destruction of what has gone before, the destruction of systems, ideas, logic, routines. It is the dynamics and explosive force of intuition; in the mind there is room for more than one ism.

Well, there you are—you, I, and everyone. Lonely, powerless, and confused. Grown older in large black space. Confused because one knows too much, understands too much, feels too much. Learning. Lonely impotence versus death. One dies alone. No one comes along. You rot until all that is left of you is empty loneliness.

It is too bad one cannot use one's talent to create trick art, that could be called art. An artist cannot be calculating, he has to paint to relieve himself of human emotions, borne by the universal forces of life. Then one does not think of making up art, of styles or directions. Something is created, something happens.

We human beings use matter between birth and death. Matter is to be used, not to possess.

1956

I never try to make a painting; it is a howl, it is naked, it is like a child, it is a caged tiger. I am the surgeon of space and paint human spaces.

My tube is like a rocket writing on its own space.

1957

Feeling directs the movement on the white surface. The unused white is beautiful, it shows the spontaneous action, the coincidences, the lines of direct expression, which works on and changes into a deeper matter.

I got acquainted with New York in 1957, mainly through the jazz musicians. I had just exhibited a series of twenty-five portraits in Paris, at the Galerie Rive Droite of Jean Larcade in the Rue du Faubourg Saint Honoré— Machteld, Lupasco, Tapié, Dr. Romiguère, Willem Sandberg, and Em. Looten—and I wanted to continue doing portraits in America.

I took over Sam Francis' studio in New York, on East 67th Street, near Madison. He was going to Japan for the first time. When I started work, Clay Felker, who worked for *Esquire*, came by, and I told him I was a great jazz fan and wanted to paint jazz musicians. He gave me a pink badge, which listed *Holiday, Esquire*, and *Life* magazines on the back. That badge was known to all doormen and police officers. It opened all doors for me—"Jazz Under the Stars" in Central Park, the Newport Jazz Festival, the Jazz Festival on Randall's Island, and the clubs where jazz was played.

I must have made a good impression on them. The musicians like me, and posed eagerly—they just dropped by the studio. Very different from France; the moment you've made some name there, it seems like you can't behave like an ordinary human being any more. Through those guys I got to know Harlem like my inside pocket—all the joints and so on. I couldn't drive yet, so they presented me with a red Alfa Romeo plus driver. I bought one of those red American caps, and went on trips all over with the photographer Tony Burnside.

He took pictures of me while I painted, a photoreportage for *Esquire*—the Dutch painter who discovered America—but it was never published, probably because it was all full of Negroes. Later they published a piece about Miles Davis, illustrated with my picture.

Great city, New York. I went to hear Charlie Mingus nearly every night. People would say he behaved maliciously, but that was not his behavior, that was his personality. One time

Dizzy came by, we had dinner and he said, "Let's go and listen to Mingus." When Dizzy entered they all came alive—those birds all play for each other, of course. Mingus left the stage, left his bass fiddle lying on the floor, and came over to us while the others were still tuning up—for them that is music too, do you understand?

He sat down at the piano, fooled around a little, and suddenly there it was—one chord, then ensemble playing—it lasted one hour—fantastic!

I myself recited a poem in English about New York in a nightclub in the Village, with rhythm background.

You can do that in New York, howl a street poem in a nightclub. That is New York. Now New York has become a cultural center. It wasn't then. I exhibited a lot, at Martha Jackson's, talked with lots of people, also for the radio. There is a whole generation of American painters now, that did not exist then. It was only a small group. I met Franz Kline, Willem de Kooning, Clyfford Still, and [Mark] Rothko—him I met the first year.

The Cedar Bar still existed in those days, no more now. I was drinking a beer one time and started a conversation with a guy in coveralls.

We went out and walked up the street together. Later I asked John Hultberg, "Who was that nice guy in the coveralls?" "That is the painter Franz Kline," he said. Later the three of us exhibited in a new gallery in Easthampton, Long Island, where we spent the summers, Kline, De Kooning, and I.

On my first visit in '57, I stayed three months. Since then I have gone practically every year; later, with Machteld, I toured for a whole year in America in a Thunderbird. I had just gotten my driver's license and conquered everything, the deserts, the Grand Canyon, Las Vegas, San Francisco, New Mexico, Mexico. We also lived in Los Angeles for a few months, in one of those big square hotels on the beach. I loved Los Angeles; it is not like anything else.

1961/62

In the beginning I painted man full of expression. Filling the canvas right to the borders, thick layers of paint. Later I discovered space, spatial space, then emptiness, empty space in which I forcefully moved the paint, action in space (human landscapes). Then I used the wet white as space-background, the unfinished space I learned about in New York, where they tear down and rebuild. In this interim people live. Now I am ready for filled-up space, where I portray man with dramatic force. The tragedy: we are in the hands of the fantastic artist of life; life itself, it lets us be born and live and is at the same time the biggest murderer, killing us irrevocably.

Action Painting

The last Sunday of November, 1958, I got a wire from Edo van Tetterode and Peter Verbruggen inviting me to Airport Zestienhoven. I was to be lifted in the air by the helicopter "Kolibrie" of the Dutch Helicopter Industry. From this position I made an action painting in black and white on large strips of white drawing paper held down on the grass with nails and stones against the draft created by the helicopter. It was the first time I appeared on camera.

I spent the spring and summer of 1961 on the 75-hectare estate of l'Abbaye de Roselande, which belongs to Jean Larcade, the director of the Paris Galerie Rive Droite, and made eighteen manhigh sculptures of the trunks of olive trees from the burned-out olive orchard. Local laborers pulled them up with their deep roots; they were rinsed and cleaned with hot water and brought back to life. After having been worked over with a chisel and ax, the trunks were painted with polyester varnish mixed with pigment—two long summers of hard work; in some cases multiple pieces formed a group. Weight 100 to 300 kilograms. They were exhibited in the Galerie Rive Droite, the Israel Museum of Jerusalem, the World's Fair in Seattle, and the Martha Jackson Gallery in New York.

If I had not become a painter, no doubt I would have become a clown. My whole life I wanted to be a clown, because when I enter a place, I make people laugh.

1968
Man is the creative space within all the complexity of infinity. That is the position from which I shall henceforth work—or rather, it is on the basis of that notion, one that is neither cerebral nor intellectual or I would be making myself a prisoner.

This experience has had a liberating effect on me and on my work. I stand aside from the opportunities and discoveries of my era in order to take advantage of *every* opportunity.

Instead of some psychological individualism, as in my early portraits, heads, the suffering, etc., I am striving for a magical individualism. Personal experience—joy, sorrow, love, hate, etc.—give way to a universal and spatial experience.

I'm beginning to paint portraits again, the human form, reliefs. The portraits and heads I began by painting had a magical look because of their features, their expressions, their vehemence, whereas now the essential thing is no longer the personality in the moment, the emotional expression.

Colored areas, spaces, juxtaposed against the background space, together make up the human figure.

Psychological individuality gives way to magic universalism. There is a huge difference between surrealism and fantastic realism. Surrealism has become a system, a new literary system, whereas fantastic realism has no system and draws upon a broader magical awareness of reality.

There is scientific evolution and there is artistic evolution, and neither can stop. Painting is a living substance.

Lima, 1976

Painting is a supple, living substance that transmits a human warmth. A spiritual warmth is a true warmth. What is most social is visible and tangible to all. It is the social organism that is alive in each of us; each of us is creative. Take, for example, the wall paintings we did in Lima, Peru. In the desert, in the slums, human contact sprang up during our work, form was transmitted, each one asimilated it and a human warmth sprang up among all the participants. By that, I mean everyone who participated in those murals. Distance, chill, both disappeared. A dimension of warmth was created, a contact that, in turn, created reasons for doing something.

It could be defined as the social contract based on inner freedom. Today we no longer see any difference between chaos and freedom; that is, today, a negative chaos holds sway over society, a social form is sinking into chaos. This is often mistaken for freedom.

As for me, I work on the basis of a positive chaos; that is, I make use of chaos. I always start with chaos and, from there, I construct a form, something emerges half way between chaos and order, and those forms, those expressions that occupy the median position represent the path of creativity. It is an energy in motion, the indeterminate gradually nurtures a certainty. Anti-art is a tactical way for us to free ourselves from the old artistic values. Many remain at that stage or fall into production. Neither cold form nor anti-art provides answers. The path of creativity is somewhere between the two.

1979

What is inspiration? I do not know. I am always inspired, that is life. The whole day is life. When I have no inspiration, I am ill, I stay in bed. I started to travel after the war—really during the war, but that was mandatory, a week here, a few months there with the farmers, hiding—to Liège in 1946, then Antwerp, Brussels, Ghent, in 1947 to Paris with Corneille, alone to Cassis, first in Suresnes at Jacobsen's in 1950.

In the Rue Santeuil until 1955; then the Rue Brezin, with the address at the Rue Santeuil used a storage until that space was torn down for horrible HLM apartments. A poor city, Paris, everything was rationed in the beginning—bread, meat, butter, sugar—but it was cheap, you could live with very little money. Went to the fleamarket at Porte de Clignancourt to buy frames secondhand and old paintings to paint over. We met Facchetti through Elly Claus, a fashion photographer, who used Michel Tapie as artistic adviser for a new gallery in the Rue de Lille. There too in 1953 I met Martha Jackson, who kept asking me to come to New York, where I went for the first time in 1957.

Amsterdam is the city of my youth, I remain an Amsterdammer—that stays in your blood, a certain Jewish humor which remains and makes you who you are. In the beginning I had no money and no space, now I have money and experience which frees me and my work. I have to release all the possibilities and discoveries of my time to be able to employ all possibilities. Instead of psychological individualism, like my early portraits, sad people, I now think of a magical individualism. The personal experience such as joy, sorrow, love and hate is replaced by a universal and spatial experience.

Again I paint portraits, man in relief. The portraits and heads I painted earlier had a magical expression, through their features, expression, and violence, while now the personal or momentary emotion is the most important. The spatial color planes are placed next to each other and over each other on a background of space, together forming man.

The psychological individualism resolves itself to make place for the magical universe. There is a big difference between Surrealism and fantastic realism. Surrealism has become

-594-

a system, a literary system. Fantastic realism doesn't admit any system, it dips into a larger magical consciousness of reality.

Love enacts itself between imagination and reality, these two poles of the human existence. On his record "Nashville Skyline," Bob Dylan sings for example: "Love is all there is, it makes the world go 'round, Love and only love, it can't be denied. No matter what you think about it/You just won't be able to do without it."

Just hearing that gives me an all-around feeling of love for life, carried on a background of emotion. All human emotions and feelings appear in my work, and therefore also in the erotic drawings and paintings—tenderness, color, aggression, straightforwardness, spontaneity, tragedy, violence, fantasy, sadism, and imagination. Man grows through his love experiences toward a more conscious plane. No morality; that is the basis of all wars. Love is not only reality; I couldn't even see my wife, Machteld, realistically; no woman is happy if she is regarded merely with realism. A woman wants to see the imagination stimulated; she has an intuitive intelligence when it comes to love. You can also make love with space, with the wind. The most violent feelings of man come from his imagination; imagination is the most important sexual organ of man; it is in his brains; it is what sets him apart from the animal, which only responds to a biological urge.

Many men never get beyond that stage. The moment they see a woman, they think with their sexual organs; they do not use their imagination. Woman to them is an object, subservient; they forget that a natural urge toward ecstasy hides in sexuality—and that is more than just orgasm.

Has a machine ever been invented that knows this mystery?

Man can try (and here I speak only for myself, I am not moralizing) to rise above the instincts, to give a more conscious form to love, for instance through seeing and giving to the other—and not just physically. Orgasm alone is not the most important, but the harmony of the physical reality and the mental imagination. Holding back and yet giving, watching and experiencing, one knowledge, one emotion, one experience, one spiritual orgasm. That is more complete, more ecstatic, more human.

In these days of political and materialistic power, man seems to forget that he was born from his mother's softest flesh. Forced into the corset of materialistic needs, threats, and superficial relationships, the wonder and miracle of life itself escapes him.

Society's conditioning has produced a dual consciousness, a dual approach to life; dual workings of the brain, feelings, and intuition have been pushed away by the intellect—orderly according to the principle of contrast: yes or no, the positive or negative, beautiful or ugly. This limitation is a great frustration; the computer, too, is adjusted this way. I reject the dual approach when I paint. Poetry needs intuition, too; physics and geometry know a multiple logic today, away from dualistic thought.

Today, people don't see the difference between chaos and freedom. Indeed, in present-day society there is a negative chaos, a social concept often called freedom, but one that becomes chaos.

I begin to work from a positive chaos. In other words, I always start with chaos and out of it I create something between chaos and order. Forms and expressions follow a middle path, the path of creativity.

It's an emotional kind of energy, a "warm" dimension. The end product emerges from vagueness. Anti-art is a tactic to get rid of old artistic values. Many artists stagnate or turn to production. The answer does not lie in some cold, carefully planned concept or in an anti-art output. The path of creativity lies somewhere between those two options.

When I paint only the present moment counts, and it is everything. Nothing exists but the here and now. No past. No future.

There are no defenses, nothing to be torn down, nothing to destroy. The canvas stands ready to concretize what lies beyond the conscious. Simply to be. Above and beyond human dualities.

It's only by working on my painting with duality that I can let my mind and body go. In my painting, form turns into vibrations, it penetrates into formless form, into the formless existence I am painting: vibrations of colors. For example, you don't immediately see the expressions of a cat I am in the process of painting.

For me, energy, form and communication constitute one thing only and the assembled forms create a face. For example, when I look at a car, it is as if I see a face which in its turn stares at me. When I walk the streets of a city, I see abstract human forms with changeable expressions, almost as if they were the shadows of themselves and of their own existence.

The oppressive sensation of a skyscraper seen as a giant being with millions of eyes that gaze at the moving mass of people, controlling it from the inside, through its intestine, similarly from the outside through its stone body, dominating its rhythm of life with a metallic, almost magical power. I see more and more the creative space of man in the infinity of the nature of this world.

As I see it, life is built up of diverse skins which have to be removed, just as you peel a banana before eating it or, better still, as you eat an artichoke, leaf after leaf, in order to arrive finally at the heart; it is only in this moment that my work is finished, totally bare and devoid of inhibitions and, if we can say it like this, of the skins of the past. It is for this reason that some people say that my work is infantile or stupid, but for me it is like life itself.

Change or changes in technique can operate in order to enlarge consciousness. By concentration and practice, it is possible to liberate the subconscious and make it known by art. Thus, the boundless forces of the imagination founded in the knowledge of the greater memory of the subconscious can express themselves.

The forms of thought seem real, fantasy takes clearer forms and the river of the subconscious begins to flow. The form of art dominates and cannot be catalogued. The result often resembles schizophrenia and is found outside the ordinary vision of the day, it is the loss of the exterior "self", of the artificial personality.

Every new method for enlarging consciousness can be clearly identified in the field of painting. The vivacious primary colours are for me the first step towards the loss of "self," the loss and the forgetting of myself and my environment. In the same moment in which my ego is eradicated and deprived of activity and intellectual values, the realization of that which is still unknown and not created, the silent «no-form» unity, emerges with the appearance of infantile schizophrenia. Only then does the indefinable begin, takes form.

1982

Evolution is necessary, self-transformation by dint of thought, mind and soul. Following such profound inner transformation, some evolution is possible. An inner evolution, not an external, material evolution. The individu-

alistic evolution leads to revolutionary states,
to transformed souls, minds and wills.

Like a relaxed human form stretched out
Across the white white of the land.
Monumental,
Frail, a huge impotent presence in the white
Landscape
Breathtaking absolute silence

A war rages within me, burning all. Now I can
Begin again.

The divested man
Awakes
Hands outstretched
White sky
The rocks shake

There is no wind
The fire has died
The flame no longer burns
The cold invades

Leaves weighted with pedantry
Hang as though dead
Under the immovable rain of ice

White is the white of the land

BIBLIOGRAPHY

1950
Christian Dotremont, *Appel*, Copenhague, Cobra Library.

1952
Michel Tapié, *Un art autre*, Paris.

1958
Marcel Brion, Sam Hunter et al., *Art Since 1945*, New York, Abrams.

1959
Charles Wentinck, *Dutch Art Since Van Gogh*, Utrecht.

1961
Willem et Jaffe Sandberg, L.C. Hans, *Contemporary Art in the Stedelijk Museum of Amsterdam*, Amsterdam.

1962
Hugo Claus, *Karel Appel, Painter*, New York, Abrams.

M. Sandberg et Straniero, *Sculptures de Karel Appel*, Turin, Fratelli Pozzo.

Jan Vrijman, *La Réalité de Karel Appel*, Amsterdam, De Bezige Bij.

A Beast Drawn Man, texte Bert Schierbeek, lithographies Karel Appel, Amsterdam, De Bezige Bij.

1963
Bert Schierbeek, *The Experimenters*, Amsterdam.
Simon Vinkenoog, *L'histoire de Karel Appel: une épreuve de perception*, Utrecht, A.W. Bruna & Zoon.

Love Song, texte de Hugo Claus, dessins Karel Appel, Amsterdam, Andreas Landshoff; New York, Abrams.

1966

R.W.D. Oxenaar, *Holland in the Art of Our Time*, Cologne, 1966.
Nello Ponente, *Modern Painting: Contemporary Trends*, Lausanne.

1968

Julien Alvard, *Karel Appel, Reliefs, 1964-1968*, Paris, Centre National d'Art Contemporain.
Peter Bellew, *Karel Appel*, Milan, Fratelli Fabbri.

1970

JAL de Meijere, *The Appels of His Eye: View of an Evolution*, Utrecht.

1971

Virtus Schade, *Cobra de la tête aux pieds*, Schelderode.
Karel Appel on Karel Appel, Amsterdam, Triton Pers.

1974

Willemijn Stokvis, *Cobra*, Amsterdam, De Bezige Bij.
Ed. Wingen, *A Look at Painters*, Amsterdam.

1977

Peter Berger, *Karel Appel*, Venlo, Pays-Bas, Van Spijk.
Ed. Wingen, *The Face of Karel Appel*, Venlo, Pays-Bas.
Ed. Wingen, *Thirty Years of Painting by Appel*, Venlo, Pays-Bas.
Éloge de la Folie, texte de Jean-Clarence Lambert,

illust. Karel Appel, Paris, Yves Rivière Arts et Métiers Graphiques.

1978
Hugo Claus, *Appel et Alechinsky*, Paris

1979
C. Honnef, *Dreizig Jahre Karel Appel*, catalogue d'exposition Bonn, Rheinisches Landesmuseum. *Appelcircus*, Abrams.

1980
Alfred Frankenstein, *Karel Appel*, New York, Abrams.

Jean-Clarence Lambert, *Karel Appel: Works on Paper*, New York, Abbeville Press.

Le Noir de l'Azur, texte de Jean-Clarence Lambert, illust. Karel Appel, Galilée Paris.

1981
E. Reinhartz-Tergau, *Het Monumentale Werk van Karel Appel*, catalogue d'exposition, La Haye, Galerie Nova Spectra.

Collectif, *Écrits sur Karel Appel*, Paris, Galilée.

1982
W.A.L. Beeren, *The New Work of Karel Appel: Paintings, 1979-1981*, catalogue d'exposition, Rotterdam, Museum Boymans-Van Beuningen.

Karel Appel: Works on Paper, catalogue d'exposition, La Haye.

Haags Gemeentemuseum

Océan blessé, poèmes, Paris, Galilée.

Ecrits sur Karel Appel, Editions Galilée, Paris, France

Street Art de Karel Appel par Pierre Restany, Editions Galilée, Paris, France, English translation,

Abbeville Press, New York.

1983

Jean-Clarence Lambert, *Cobra* Paris/Anvers, Ed. du Chêne/Fonds Mercator; New York, Abbeville Press. *Portfolio with Prints and Poems*, textes de Kenneth White et Karel Appel, Paris, François Benichou.

1984

New York, la ville des villes, texte de Edgard Morin, illust. Karel Appel, Harriet de Visser, Paris, Galilée (bilingue anglais/français).

Flash Art, Edition Français: *Karel Appel*—Interview avec Jean Pierre Bordaz, printemps 1984

Tema celeste, Riusta d'arte contemporanea: *La Dimensione Del Sentimento di Karel Appel*

Artiscribe nr. 45: *Appel Now* by Rasaad Jamie (Cover Artscribe by Karel Appel)

1985

Propos en liberté de Karel Appel, entretiens avec André Verdet et Frédéric de Towarnicki, Paris, Galilée.

Les Fenêtres de Karel Appel, poèmes d'André Verdet, Paris, Galilée.

Big Appel and the Cobra paintings, Robert Pincus Whitten, James Goodman Gallery

1986

Sculpture work, P. Restany, F. de Towarnicki and Allen Ginsberg, Abbeville Press, New York

Karel Appel recent paintings, Sam Hunter, catalogue Marisa del Re Gallery

1987

Nocturne de San Ildefonso, poème d'Octavio Paz,

illust. Karel Appel, Paris, Galilée (bilingue espagnol/français).

Karel Appel, 40 ans de peinture, sculpture & dessin, Editions Galilée, Paris.

1988

Karel Appel — Early Works 1937-1957, text by Michel Ragon, Edition Galileé, Paris Meulenhof/Landshof, Amsterdam.

Karel Appel — Œuvre sur papièr, Editions Cercle D'Art, Paris and Editiones Poligrafa, Barcelona.

1989

Dupe of Being, edited by Roland Hagenberg, Edition Lafayette, New York.

COLLECTIONS

Albright-Knox Art Gallery, Buffalo
Art Gallery of Ontario, Toronto
The Baltimore Museum of Art, Baltimore
Boymans-Van Beuningen Museum, Rotterdam
Carnegie Institute, Pittsburgh
Centraal Museum der Gemeente Utrecht, Utrecht
The Chrysler Museum, Norfolk, Virginie
Dayton Art Institute, Dayton, Ohio
Frans Hals Museum, Haarlem
Galerie des 20. Jahrhunderts, Berlin Ouest
Galleria d'Arte Moderna, Turin
Gemeente Museum, Breda, Pays-Bas
Haags Gemeentemuseum, La Haye
Hamilton Museum, Hamilton, Canada
Institute of Contemporary Art, Boston
Koninklijke Museum voor Schone Kunsten, Anvers
Kunstgalleri, Aarhus, Danemark
Kunsthaus Zurich, Zurich
Kunstmuseum Winterthur, Winterthur
Los Angeles County Museum of Art, Los Angeles
Louisiana Museet, Humlebaek, Danemark
Moderna Museet, Stockholm
Montreal Museum of Fine Arts, Montreal
Musée d'Art Moderne, Bruxelles
Museo de Arte Moderna, Mexico
Museo de Bellas Artes, Caracas
Museu de Arte Moderna, São Paulo
Musée National d'Art Moderne, Centre
Georges-Pompidou, Paris
Museum of Fine Arts, Boston
Museum of Modern Art, New York
Museum voor Schone Kunsten, Gand
National Gallery of Canada, Ottawa
Nationalmuseet, Copenhague
Phoenix Art Museum, Phoenix
San Francisco Museum of Modern Art,
San Francisco
Solomon R. Guggenheim Museum, New York
Sonja Henie-Neils Onstad Foundation, Oslo
Stanford University Museum and Art Gallery,
Stanford, Californie
Stedelijk Museum, Amsterdam
Stedelijk Van Abbe Museum, Eindhoven
Tate Gallery, Londres
University Art Museum, Berkeley
University of Arizona Museum of Art, Tucson
Vancouver Art Gallery, Vancouver, Canada
Vassar College Art Gallery, Poughkeepsie
Walker Art Center, Minneapolis